MEMOIRS OF A RECOVERED MUSICIAN

HOOKED
ON A
HORN

Gene Hull

© Copyright 2005 by Gene Hull.
Second Edition, 2006
All rights reserved. No part of this publication may be reproduced, stored in a retrieval system, or transmitted, in any form or by any means, electronic, mechanical, photocopying, recording, or otherwise, without the written prior permission of the author.

Note for Librarians: A cataloguing record for this book is available from Library and Archives Canada at www.collectionscanada.ca/amicus/index-e.html
ISBN 1-4120-6721-9

Printed in Victoria, BC, Canada. Printed on paper with minimum 30% recycled fibre.
Trafford's print shop runs on "green energy" from solar, wind and other environmentally-friendly power sources.

Offices in Canada, USA, Ireland and UK

Book sales for North America and international:
Trafford Publishing, 6E–2333 Government St.,
Victoria, BC V8T 4P4 CANADA
phone 250 383 6864 (toll-free 1 888 232 4444)
fax 250 383 6804; email to orders@trafford.com

Book sales in Europe:
Trafford Publishing (UK) Limited, 9 Park End Street, 2nd Floor
Oxford, UK OX1 1HH UNITED KINGDOM
phone +44 (0)1865 722 113 (local rate 0845 230 9601)
facsimile +44 (0)1865 722 868; info.uk@trafford.com

Order online at:
trafford.com/05-1632

10 9 8 7 6 5

*There are only two kinds of music –
  good music and bad music.*
                    Duke Ellington

*When you put in good things you didn't do,
  and leave out the bad things you did,
  that's a memoir.*
                    Will Rogers

GENE HULL

To my family.

AUTHOR'S INTRODUCTION

The danger in writing a memoir, whether or not you're famous, is that you can easily slide into a mush pit of truth versus fiction—and I don't mean just changing a few names for the sake of privacy. To maintain interest, possibly to capture a wider audience, you may be tempted to get too creative.

This happens not suddenly, but by degrees. First you add more color to reality. Then you may begin to juice up the facts, fudge a little truth here and there. Eventually the memoir can evolve into gross exaggeration, until at length you're on the brink of outright fabrication. It happens.

So what, you say. What harm? Who would know? The answer is: you will, and so will somebody else. Shouldn't the public be protected?

Wouldn't it be fun if the conscience of the memoir writer could burst in, take over at the precise moment creativity gets out of hand and rein it in, thereby setting the record straight immediately? The memoir could then be rescued from its possible credibility deficit; the reader would be saved from being hoodwinked and the author might still be a candidate for eternal salvation.

Accordingly, I've invited my big-mouth conscience to have a seat at my shoulder and oversee the writing of this memoir. As a result, you will discover this voice sometimes rearing its nosey head just as the going gets irresistibly good, necessitating the need for a bit of rewrite here and there. Fear not, however. The real truth turns out to be more interesting than what might have been passed off as fact.

CONTENTS

Author's INTRODUCTION

Prologue – STUPIDONE   9

1.   ROOTS   36
2.   AT THE LYRIC   42
3.   MAYBE SOMDAY   55
4.   THE RITZ   64
5.   ME AND MY SHADOW   74
6.   IS EVERYBODY HAPPY?   79
7.   THE AUDITION   85
8.   SATURDAY NIGHT IN TEXAS   94
9.   RHAPSODY IN BLUE   108
10.   THE MUSICIANS CLUB   117
11.   WHITE FLASH   127
12.   THE JAZZ GIANTS   139
13.   THE NEWPORT JAZZ FESTIVAL   151

14.	*LENNIE*	164
15.	*THE ICONS*	170
	Basie and Sarah	
	Sir Duke	
	Stan Kenton	
	Woody Herman	
	Dave Brubeck	
16.	*"FATHER OF EIGHT, ODs"*	184
17.	*SOMETIMES I HATED LYRICS*	192
18.	*THE BAND PLAYED ON*	200
19.	*LAS VEGAS*	211
20.	*MEETING ELVIS*	220
21.	*IT'S GREAT, BUT…*	226
22.	*SEGUE*	232
23.	*VOYAGE*	240
24.	*CODA*	248
	WITH GRATITUDE	255
	ABOUT THE AUTHOR	257
	POST SCRIPT	260

GENE HULL

Prologue

STUPIDONE

I wondered if anyone would be there to meet me. I hoped not.

The teak railings had crusted with salt during the ship's transatlantic crossing. I could feel the grittiness on my forearms as I leaned against the Lido Deck railing, hands clasped, looking down onto the pier of the terminal. It was eight o'clock in the morning. The ocean liner S.S. Independence had arrived in Naples as scheduled, June 10, 1968.

Already the heat of the Mediterranean sun was oozing sweat from the bare backs of longshoremen on the pier. The day promised to develop into a swelterer—not unusual weather in southern Italy at this time of year. But for me the day would prove to be anything but 'not unusual.'

The long heavy hawser lines, securing both ends of the ship to the quay, seemed almost alive, stretched out like tentacled strands of twisted muscle wrapped around the steel mooring posts rooted in the concrete dock. Everything has a purpose, even squat little mooring posts. We couldn't have docked without them.

From my vantage point, I had a good view of the area. Except for stevedores, who were off-loading baggage with disinterest, the pier was quiet, almost deserted. Good. I didn't really want to meet my Italian relatives anyway. As a matter of fact, I dreaded it. Not that I was a snob, but they were peasants, and I was only doing this for my grandfather. Actually, it was my mother who had asked me, "Please do this for Grampa."

"Aw Mom, I'd really rather not."

"He's an old man," she said. "It would make him so happy. And he did so much for you when you were little."

"Like what? Give me gruff haircuts and yell at me? I really have no desire to meet his family when I'm in Italy. They don't even speak English."

"Anna does. And they are your cousins. Aren't you even a little curious to know about them?'

"Not really. Why should I want to meet them? I have nothing in common with them."

"Well, they're my family too," she said, and I think it'd be good for you to meet them."

"Mom, we're in Naples for only one day; and that's my chance to see Italy."

"Well, it's something you should do," she said. "and it's important to me."

I thought about that for a moment. Important to me. She had never used that trump card before. "Okay," I said.

After the dissolution of the 17-piece Jazz Giants band, I formed a commercial, if somewhat esoteric, entertainment-oriented trio, GK-3. In order to work steadily, I started to travel again. It had been twelve years since I last went on the road.

The new group produced a unique sound with electric flute, electric chordovox, and percussion. Ken Duca played chordovox with amazing facility and was my partner in the group. Billy Barrick was our percussionist. I doubled flute and saxophone. Our repertoire encompassed a wide range of interesting music, from jazz to pop to classical, all peppered with extemporaneous improvisational inserts. We sang also. The trio was never out of work. We had been booked to play for the ship's summer Atlantic crossing, its Mediterranean cruises, the return crossing to New York, and a few Caribbean cruises.

The booking afforded an excellent opportunity to meet people and make contacts. I was determined to make the best of it. Now in my mid-thirties, I was in a hurry; I had no time for casual meetings with distant relatives, especially those of my grandfather. They couldn't further my career. Every minute had to count, had to payoff in some way. After all, I had a career to build and a family to support and I was trying to make up for lost but necessary time I had spent at home for the past several years. So I figured meeting those relatives would not only be a distraction, it would take time away from something more necessary, whatever that might be. Besides, I just didn't feel like seeing them.

My maternal grandfather, Antonio Persico, came to America from Sorrento seventy-five years before, and now at ninety-seven, he had just retired as the barber of his own shop. The whole town of Bridgeport knew *Tony the Barber*. His shop had been on the same corner, Railroad Avenue and Park, for over seventy years. He saved every penny, sending his relatives money every month, never missing, except during the war years of the Forties, when mail to and from Europe was iffy at best.

From time to time, various generations of the clan would send back pictures to him of what they had been able to buy with the money Papa Tony had sent to them -a new refrigerator, the floor tile they installed, a hot water heater, new toilets, a new iron, a TV. Once they enclosed a picture of a pink pig they had added to the stock of animals actually living for a time on the ground floor of their three-story hillside house.

I could understand why Papa Tony was like a God to their whole village. He had made good in America and hadn't forgotten his family. They worshiped his name. To me, he was just this gruff, little old irritable grandfather who spoke broken

English. I remembered how 'vibration' somehow mutated to 'volabrash' when he said it. He had little sense of eating etiquette, slurping his soup, chewing open-mouthed, picking his teeth at the table. And you could forget about 'please pass' the whatever.

When Antonio came to America as a young man in the late 1800's, the Italians were at the low end of the pecking order. A hundred years before, immigrating Germans had faced similar circumstances, taking the lowest paying laborer jobs, gradually working their way up through the social system. The massive Irish immigrations of the mid-1800's produced the same conditions, only worse, especially in over-crowded cities of the northeast. By the late 1800's, when it was the Italians' turn, resourceful Antonio, sizing up the situation soon after he arrived, passed himself off initially as a Frenchman to a pretty, young Irish immigrant, Ella Lillis, my future maternal grandmother, who, apparently not knowing the difference between French and Italian, believed him. They fell in love and soon were married.

Antonio may have never picked up polite table manners, but he obviously knew how to survive in a hostile environment and how to get things done. I respected his no-nonsense practicality. But why didn't he speak better English after so many years here? Why did he walk around the house in wintertime in long underwear, wearing a bowler hat and black, high-button shoes? Why did he yell at me so much? Why didn't he ever read books? Why couldn't he be like other people on our street? Why did the Irish neighborhood kids call me "Wop," "Guinea," "Dago," and "Grease Ball, " when I was a little kid? I'd always stick up for my grandfather, but inside I blamed him for being so foreign.

"Mom," I'd tell her, "Grampa thinks college is for people who don't know how to work with their hands."

Her response was always the same, "Your grandfather is a good man. He's worked hard all his life and helps others. He's never had an education and doesn't know anything about college."

When she told him I had been elected President of my class, he said " Hum, how mucha da money he make-a for that?"

He just wasn't an American in my eyes, whatever that meant in those days. After all, how was I ever going to be a famous musician if my grandfather could hardly speak English? Ethnic diversity was not a chic social advantage in those days. I was ashamed of him, and sadly, because of him, I was ashamed of my own part-Italian heritage.

One Memorial Day, at my mother's request, my brother and I had agreed to help our grandfather paint his barbershop. I was a wise-ass college student of twenty at the time and a precocious musician, with somewhat of that screw-you-I'm-a-jazz-player attitude. I dipped the brush into the paint bucket and slapped the thick, fresh white mixture onto the pattern-stamped tin wall covering, spreading it quickly with long, broad strokes. It splattered a bit. But I didn't care. It felt good. It wouldn't take long. And I liked doing something physical. This would be a kick, I thought.

"No, No! Stupidone! Too mucha da paint!" my grandfather snarled from across the three-barber-chair shop, after only two dips of my brush. "Whatsa matter you? You gotta no brains? Justa washa da face."

He was a frugal, hardworking man, and obviously a thorough paint covering was not what he had in mind for the walls. My brother Duane just chuckled. To me it was more like whitewashing than painting. It wasn't a pleasant day. I never was asked, nor did I volunteer, to paint again. I could still hear my grandfather's gruff rebukes from that day. He had called me stupid, and that galled me.

I never got close to my grandfather. I couldn't relate to his foreign-ness, or the barbershop, or the way he reported to my mother, "Say, Marguerite, the boy fell asleep with the radio on again last night." As far as I was concerned, he was impatient, always needed to control a situation and had to be the center of attention. Besides, I hated the smells in the kitchen when my mother cooked up one of his favorite meals, a conglomeration of smelly onions, green peppers, beet greens, red peppers, peas and potatoes. "Peasant food. It really stinks up the house," I used to say to her.

Looking down from the deck of the ship onto the sprawling pier below, I saw four people, three women and a man, standing almost directly below me, searching the faces of the few passengers gathered at the railing to get a morning first look at Naples. The young man wore a tight, brown jacket and a wide, floral tie. He sported a narrow-brimmed, old fedora, and he seemed comfortable with that. The three young women were wearing bright print dresses and flat sandals. Each was holding a balloon, apparently just as people had done decades ago to catch the attention of a relative arriving as an immigrant in New York from the old country. I was aware of the old custom. My grandfather had told me about it years ago, how immigrants, packed on the decks of arriving ships, searched across the terminal for relatives holding balloons. People hadn't done that in many decades. And yet there they were with balloons—the only people meeting the ship. I hoped these weren't my relatives. Balloons, yet.

I tried not to look at them. As a matter of fact, I deliberately turned my head away because I didn't want to make eye contact, just in case they were my cousins. But one of the women caught my passing glance, and before I could avert it, she yelled up, squinting, and shading her eyes from the hot morning sun pouring out of the east over the top of the ship, "Hey! You know Jen Hall?"

Wishing they weren't, but realizing oh my God, they're my cousins, I cupped my mouth with both hands and targeted my reply down to them, "I'm Gene Hull."

With that, the three women began to scream with delight and jump up and down. They joined hands, formed a circle, included the reluctant young man, and danced about wildly happy-faced.

Were they for real? I realized how embarrassing it would be to tell my new friends on board that I had found my Italian peasant cousins—or rather, they had found me—and they were even worse than I had expected.

"I'll be down in a little while," I yelled, and walked away from the railing. Mom, how could you do this to me?

I eased my way back across Lido Deck to the outdoor table where I had left my Waspy friends, the Washington, DC crowd. Shaking my head in disbelief, I sat down to finish my breakfast.

"You won't believe the scene down on the pier," I said. "There are only four people waiting for the ship. And guess what? They're my cousins. Well, two of the women are. And they're actually holding balloons! Can you believe that?" I recounted the story of my mother's request. I told them about my grandfather and my distant Italian cousins. (In the course of revealing my personal history, I never did mention that I had eight children. They probably would have said. 'What the hell are you doing here?' I decided they didn't need to know. At the time I considered the omission to be less than honest. I'm still not proud of that.)

They were amused and kidded me for having such unsophisticated, if colorful, relatives, and even for being part 'peasant Italian.' I laughed right along with them and allowed as how I was 'only one-quarter Italian.'

Later my cousins explained that the reason they were the only visitors on the pier was that they had to apply at the Maritime Magistrate Offices many weeks before in order to get special passes to go inside the iron gates to meet the ship. Whenever a passenger liner from America was in port in those days, no one was allowed on the docks without special permission. Too many potential stowaways tried to get on board.

When I had signed a contract with American-Isbrantson Lines for my group to perform on the S.S. Independence, letters had flown back and forth between Italy and my grandfather. It was soon agreed that the cousins, Anna, Gina, and their friend Marguerite, would meet me in Naples when the ship docked there. My grandfather was overjoyed at the prospect. They would take me to visit his old home near Sorrento for the day, and bring me back to the ship in late afternoon. I spoke no Italian and really didn't know much about my relatives. But what I did know held little interest for me. Certainly not in my league. But okay, it's only for one day. I can do this.

I had made friends easily during the crossing. Each night our lounge was the main gathering place for entertainment and dancing. Our music was varied with a lively potpourri of light classical, jazz and pop tunes. It was a hit with the passengers. By the fifth day at sea we had developed a following. They'd begun to request certain arrangements we had played earlier and had already become their favorites.

One of our newfound fans was a former U.S. diplomatic courier, Bob La Plante, who played fluegal horn, poorly, if with conviction. He loved to sit in with our trio and jam the same two songs every night, flubbing the fourth note of "I Can't Get Started" with such regularity that it was difficult for me to keep from grimacing. I tried to keep my reaction from showing. His encore was always "When The Saints Go Marching In." This tired evergreen held no interest for me either. But somehow, when he played it, it became fun again. Perhaps it was because he appeared to be living his fantasy, playing with a professional band. Music was pure fun for him. What a concept.

Gretchen, his beautiful young German wife, told stories of the intense days in post war Germany, of how her parents had forbidden her to see him because he was an American with a dangerous job steeped in foreign intrigue and Cold War skullduggery. When he was a courier, a classified pouch was always handcuffed to his wrist until he delivered it, no matter where it had to go. Apparently more than one courier had been found dead, missing a hand severed at the wrist. It was real-life. Not the movies. I was impressed.

Then there was twenty-eight-year-old Rosie, the shapely brunette, a State Department attaché, returning from a Kansas home vacation to her assignment in Barcelona. She had already attracted the undivided attention of the ship's dashing 1st Officer.

The 'friends' group also included Polish Count and Countess, or so they said, Isadore and Ilona Gavlicki, who lived in New York, and were on their way to Italy, visiting friends with villas in Rome, Tuscany and Portofino. Isadore wore a green eye-patch, had one wooden leg, and a huge, warm laugh. The Countess, as everyone called her, was the epitome of old-world charm, always perfectly made up and tastefully dressed with the quiet elegance of the European old riche. They were of that class for whom 'summer' was a verb. They fascinated me. I always felt like I should bow when they came by.

Most intriguing was the group of young sophisticates from Washington, D.C., with their cocktail parties, elaborate dinners, and expensive cigars. They danced late every night — the men in white dinner jackets, the ladies in their Emilio Pucci multi-colored long dresses. They were beautiful and handsome and made a fuss over our music. I fell in with this crowd naturally.

To top it off, the passenger list included a handful of movie stars going to a film festival in Nice. Jim Nabors, who played the well-known TV character Gomer Pyle, had hiked the Rock of Gibraltar with me when the ship stopped there a week before, chatting about his TV life and about his home in Hawaii. He said his best friend, Carol Burnett, was his neighbor. I felt important knowing him.

The whole cruise experience was exhilarating, a far cry from playing in smoky dives, Holiday Inns and roadhouse cafés. I tried to fit in with the worldly and wealthy. I was genuinely impressed with their stories, their almost reverent adherence to cocktail hour (something new for me) and the time they had for leisure. I was always doing something to get ahead or pay bills, so it all was very sophisticated to me. They didn't seem to need anything, and I was afflicted with an entertainer's need for applause and acceptance.

"Gene," said Ned, one of the haughty Staunton twins from D.C., who seemed to have been everywhere and done everything, "Why are you wasting time with relatives? Sorrento is a long drive from here. You might miss the ship. After all, Genie Boy, they're only peasants; you said so yourself. We're all going down to Pompeii to see the ruins, and then have lunch at the Grande Excelsior Vittoria. You're welcome to join us."

I thought about it. I would have loved to hang out with this crowd. I didn't want to appear unappreciative, and I did have a hard time saying no sometimes.

"Thanks, Ned. I'd like to. But as I told you, I promised my mother." An uncomfortable hole in the conversation developed.

"Oh, it'll be good for a giggle," gushed Trisha, breaking the silence, timing my rescue with the confident aplomb that comes so easily to the privileged. She was a sincere, twenty-two year old Washington society debutante, very sweet, with lovely brown eyes, full lips, slender hips, and a genuine, warm smile—

Ned's girlfriend, I assumed. *Oh my.* I was rather taken with her myself.

"You can tell us all about it when you get back, Gene", she added very upbeat. And then turning to the others cheerfully, "Let's all meet here for cocktails at six, and Gene will tell about his day. Okay everybody?" How gay. How fun.

"Right," the rest agreed. "At six then."

"Okay. See you later everybody," I said, and I left the breakfast table, "And don't worry. I'll be back in time."

I was always on time for everything in those days. In fact, I was usually early. I began to think about the day ahead of me. Ned was right; it probably would be a long drive. I knew Italy didn't have 'interstates' yet. I wondered if I would make it back before the ship sailed at 6:00 PM. Missing the ship for an employee was serious; it had said so in the Maritime Articles when I signed-on to the ship. And what about my luggage? My clothes? My instruments? And the money? What would happen to the musicians in my trio? Most likely I would have to pay their fares back to New York at the least. I looked at my watch as I made my way down the six decks to the crew gangway, determined not to let the time get away from me.

I stepped down the gangway. Once on the pier, I was surrounded and warmly hugged by my cousins Anna and Gina and their friend Marguerite, as though I were a long lost prodigal whatever. Anna, who was around my age, spoke English fairly well. Introductions followed. The guy in the tight clothes was Franco, Marguerite's boy friend. The owner of an old car, a small, once-green, four door Fiat, he had been cajoled by the girls into driving to Napoli to meet "Cousin Geno from America," Papa Tony's grandson. I sensed a proud indifference from Franco, as if he really didn't give a hoot for Geno or America. He would rather have been taking a nap, I guessed, probably with Marguerite, who was a fun-loving, ripe twenty-two year old, threatening to spill out of her low-cut summer dress at any moment. The possibility of this kept Franco's attention. Mine, too.

As we approached the waiting Fiat, the four of them circled around it, bumping each other like Keystone Kops, trying to decide who would sit where. It was finally settled with Franco and Marguerite in the front seat, and Gina, Anna and I squeezing into the back. Franco took off his jacket and tie and rolled up his shirtsleeves past his elbows, as if preparing for physical labor. He handed his hat to Marguerite.

Once underway, he was in his element. He knifed and zigzagged through the chaotic madness of Naples traffic with its din of beeps and honks, weird midget cars, buzzing hoards of Vespa scooters (the kamikaze motorati) and a multitude of trucks of every description, all racing wildly, like the start of a land purchase stampede, from one traffic light to the next at unrestrained speeds. Once the race halted at a light, drivers ignored each other but revved up motors in preparatory challenge for the next takeoff.

I saw that crossing the wide city thoroughfares of Naples, Italy's second largest city—home of the pizza, Sophia Loren, "O Sole Mio" and Mt. Vesuvius—could be a death-defying experience for pedestrians, who automatically thumbed their noses or flipped a bird with fully bended elbows at drivers who had barely missed them. Drivers often shared such pleasantries, adding an unabridged, one or two–word piece of their Italian minds. It never seemed to bother anyone for more than a moment.

Franco was no exception. He swore and gestured heatedly at other drivers, none of whom, including him, seem to take it personally. Next to Franco Marguerite sat with her flowery frock pulled up well past her knees. After all, it was a hot day and the car had no air conditioning. Franco was in heat himself and couldn't keep his eyes or his hands off her. In the narrow back seat the two other women and I squished together like an upright stack of folding chairs — Gina on the left, Anna in the middle and I on the right. With elbows tightly drawn in against our stomachs, deep breathing was something not to be taken for granted and required some instinctive compromising.

The car cleared the city and headed out to the two-lane highway that led down the coast to Sorrento, the famous town scenically perched on the edge of the Mediterranean about thirty miles away at the southern end of the great Bay of Naples.

Once on the road, Franco accelerated the Fiat to full gale speed, obviously enjoying the trip, with windows open, hair blowing, and on-coming traffic whizzing past us. The narrow road wound along the perimeter of the magnificent Bay of Naples, cut into the side of mountainous terrain that rose in a steep grade from the sea. From my seat I could look almost straight down the 100-foot cliff on my right to the blue Mediterranean below. Incredibly beautiful. *But oh my God, this road is narrow.*

Anna could see my concern. "Geno," she said, "Franco has-a drive dis-a road many times. Eat's okay. Notta to worry."

"All right, Anna. But we're going pretty fast. And this is a very curvy road."

I looked at my watch again, placated for the moment. She repeated this exchange in Italian to the others. They laughed and smiled at me, and patted my arm — or wherever they could touch me—as if to say, 'That's okay, we'll take care of you,'little Geno.' Even Franco thought it was funny and turned around to reassure me, shaking my hand while steering with the other.

"Look out, "I yelled, as we lurched around a curve and headed straight for a slow, oncoming truck full of chicken crates in the other lane. Franco swerved suddenly back to his side of the road, swore, and yelled out his window at the other driver as the vehicles barely missed each, adding an Italian gesture which probably translated into: 'What the hell's the matter with you?' Looking out the back window as we sped away, I saw that the truck had veered off the road and was halted on a precarious tilt part way up an embankment. Several crates had slipped off the back and chickens were squawking all over the road.

And so went this frenetic drive to Sorrento. Anna would converse with me in English, and then repeat what had been said in Italian for the others. They in turn would nod understandingly. Several times Franco turned around and said something in Italian to me, whereupon I would yell and point wide-eyed at an oncoming vehicle, which somehow Franco managed to miss. *I'm going to die. I know it.* I stared at my watch. An hour had already passed. This is not good.

Anna had spent a year in the United States when she was thirty, and she told me she didn't like the phoniness and the fast life in the States. "People in America don't know how to live, Geno. Run, run. Always run. No relax. No enjoy. That's no living. The only thing they do right is know how to make money!"

She had a point, and of course she repeated it to the others. They agreed with knowing nods, which I took to mean, 'Yeah, that's for sure.'

They respected the fact that Americans seemed to know how to make money. And I didn't contest it. Someday I hoped to make plenty myself, when my music was recorded, and I was famous.

By 11:30AM we were on the outskirts of Sorrento. I looked at my watch and made a mental note: we'd better leave by 3:00 PM at the latest in order to be back in time. To the right I could see the Isle of Capri just off the coast, gleaming like a soft, green, hilly jewel in the mid-day Mediterranean golden glow. What a sight, mountained, lagooned, terraced, treed, and flowered. It looked so inviting and dramatic with its tall cliffs rising right out of the sea. I could understand why Roman emperors and the gods of Roman mythology had 'lived' there.

"Capri," said Anna, pointing out the car window past me, accenting the first syllable. "I have-a boutique there, but I tooka today off to be with you."

"You do? You did?" I said. She nodded, and we continued into the busy, picturesque, narrow streets of Sorrento. Kids were playing everywhere, oblivious of the real world. Neighbors leaned out of windows and chatted across alleys. Vendors sold fruits and vegetables from their carts with the machismo of serious bankers. And everywhere waves of music from radios and record players crossed paths with double and triple aural exposures, morphing into a musical tapestry that I found at once stimulating and enchanting. Sorrento was charming, an easy little town of incredible beauty. And despite its unpretentiousness, I could sense the people were proud and took themselves seriously.

There was a gentle, uncomplicated quality about the place that made me feel relaxed. I loved the mélange of aromas. Smells of fresh flowers, fish, mint, pasta sauces, animals, garlic, pastries and fresh bread wafted into my nostrils.

The rusty trusty Fiat crept along steadily. I checked my watch again. It was about that time that Marguerite began hugging Franco around the neck, practically sitting on his lap. "Franco, Franco, *mi amore!*" she said. I guessed she was grateful to him for using his car. After all, the four of them had arisen at 4:00 AM to drive to Napoli, so they would be there when the ship came in. And this was probably her way of rewarding Franco, for the time being at least. Or maybe her hormones were just responding impulsively to the romantic Sorrento environment. Soon her hugs were followed with loud kisses, a long, wet-tongued one slurping into his right ear. And as she apparently slipped a hand between his legs, Franco hit a goat. Ka-thlump! Someone screamed. Everything stopped, including the car.

People who were going about their business poured out onto the narrow side street, yelling and pointing, all of them running to see what was going on.

More shouting and *"mamma mia's"* followed. Some of the old ladies in the swelling crowd held their heads in both hands. A round, gray-haired matron railed at Franco, who was still sitting in the car, regarding her with indifference. After all, *he* had a car. Another woman, short and plump, with all the tact of a drill sergeant, scolded Marguerite, who had jumped out to pet the poor goat lying injured on the ground. Children started to kick the car and beat against it with a switch of twigs, as if it were a bad car. Anna and I managed to wriggle ourselves out of the back seat. It was an Italian street scene from a Rossini opera and getting more commotional by the moment. A butcher came out of his shop and shook a cleaver at Franco. A man who looked as if he could be a farmer threw up both his arms and cursed in the local dialect *"Ba fenabala"*. Suddenly Anna cried out, *"Stazitto! Solito! Silenzio!"*

Quiet descended. When she was sure she had their attention, Anna explained dramatically that, "This", turning to me, gesticulating with an out-stretched arm, "is Papa Tony's grandson from America, our cousin Geno, and we are on our way to our village, Masa Lubrenza, just two miles away." She added that she would gladly "pay for the goat."

"Ooooooh," they said, nodding slowly in unison. *"Ahh. ce, senorina, ah, ce.* Papa Tony." They nodded toward me and backed away.

It seemed to me that they were unusually respectful. And then I remembered that Robert Kennedy had been assassinated only a few days before while walking through the kitchen of a Los Angeles Hotel with his entourage. The world was shocked by the event. Another Kennedy killed. Italians, who especially loved the Kennedys, took the news extremely hard. To them the Kennedys were larger than life, the world's royalty. It was as if they had lost a beloved star of their own. Many sobbed openly when the ship had stopped at Sardinia the day before. American passengers were greeted solicitously and received heartfelt condolences from the people. Most residents wore black armbands in sympathy, and pictures of the Kennedys with black ribbons on the frames were posted outside many of the local shops. A large condolence book to be sent to Ethel Kennedy was displayed for all to sign. Their warmth and concern for us touched me.

So Anna had said the right words: Papa Tony and America. It worked. She gave some money to the lady of generous circumference, who immediately stopped complaining. We got back in the car. Franco steered around the fallen goat — some barefooted kids were trying to milk it– and we rumbled out of town at about five-miles-an-hour onto a dirt road that led to the little village just ahead.

As our car approached Massa Lubrenza, I saw a crowd of several hundred people gathered at the base of the fifty-or-so steps that led up the grassy hill to the Persico compound. The village had a population of about four hundred. Apparently most, including the parish priest, had turned out to see Papa Tony's grandson. Everyone cheered as I stepped out. My grandfather's ninety-three-year-old sister, the surviving matriarch of the clan, Emilianna, was standing at the head of the group in a place of honor, a wrinkled, wizened figure wearing a long black dress, high-button black shoes and a black shawl draped over her head and shoulders. She blessed me then held me at arm's length to get a good look. "Antonio, Antonio," she said, as she hugged me and wept, apparently thinking I was her long-lost-to-America brother. It embarrassed me.

Anna took my hand and led me to the steps. I kept looking around in all directions. I could see Sorrento and beautiful Capri out in the sea. To the north, a few miles off, loomed Mt. Vesuvius, a smoking giant, hovering over its dominion like a mythic dinosaur warning the wary not to ignore it. I could even see Pompeii, where life had stopped instantly in 73 AD, buried in a blizzard of molten ash from the Vesuvius eruption. Ahead, at the crest of the hill, stood what used to be their farmhouse and now was an impressive, large, three-story stone house with two pink marble pillars straddling the front entrance.

We didn't go right in. Instead, we by-passed the entrance and walked around to the back. The hilly acreage there was filled with trees—lemons, figs, pears and peaches. Grape arbors drooped, burdened with purple bunches. Adjacent to the flower gardens was a small barn for the few cows, goats and pigs, which obviously were no longer welcome in the house. Three other substantial houses nestled comfortably among the tall pines on the ten acres of hilltop land. I looked around. My grandfather's family lives in this private compound of big houses, atop a beautiful spread of land across from the Isle of Capri, overlooking Sorrento and the blue Mediterranean, with a breathtaking view of Mt. Vesuvius. They're happy and loving and gracious. This place is a paradise. And I'm looking down on them?

We walked every step of the land, escorted by the whole entourage who clearly wanted to show their respect for "Papa Tony" and for me. They behaved as if following a dignitary, with slow strides, hands clasped behind their backs, nodding to each other each time I reacted to whatever Anna pointed out to me. She explained who lived where, pointed out the tree that 'Papa Tony' himself had planted eighty years before, and the grape vines and fruit trees he had cultivated. I marveled at the oversize, luscious-looking citrus — unpicked prizes. Anna led me to the wine cellar my grandfather had dug into the side of a hill where he had made wines from the grapes he had grown.

I was impressed and humbled. As a matter of fact, I was beginning to feel ashamed. I realized how wrong I had been about my Italian relatives and my grandfather. I really didn't know them and I had pre-judged them. I had no idea of how giving and warm these people were, how they felt about my grandfather and how much they honored him this day by showing me such respect.

Then suddenly it struck me. I can't be late for the ship. I looked at my watch. It was almost 2 PM.

"Shouldn't we start back to Naples now, Anna?"

"Oh no, Geno. We have a bigga luncha for you. Notta to worry."

Notta to worry? Hum. We went into the house. A long, polished, veneer wooden table with a green oilcloth cover had been set up in the large, pink tiled kitchen on the second floor. Its generous space indicated it was the most important room in the house.

I was asked to sit at one end of the table. Anna sat next to me. Emiliana was at the opposite end. My cousins and other important members of the families joined us at the table, twelve in all. They had taken the day off from their jobs to meet Geno. Several of the clan's younger women, who did not sit at the table with us, served course after course of superb dishes—pastas with red sauce, tender beefsteaks with succulent mushroom gravy, pork chops stuffed with spinach, sensuously seasoned chicken legs and breasts, fresh green vegetables, casseroles, salads, fruits, and creamy potatoes, all nurtured and grown on their land—served with a delicious red wine they had made from grapes they had cultivated. Everyone sipped the wine, cut with soda water. A tall blue vase filled with a colorful mixture of fresh garden flowers decorated the table.

Anna told them about her conversations with "Geno" on their ride from Napoli and her comment that Americans didn't know how to relax but did know how to make money. They loved it and voiced their strong agreement. *"Ahh.. Ceeee"*, they said.

GENE HULL

All through lunch the people of the village lined up outside the house. In single file they entered through the front door into the kitchen, walked around the table to the place where I was seated and were introduced to me by Anna. I stood for each introduction, shook hands warmly with each person, then sat down again. Between greetings I managed to chew a few more mouthfuls of the delicious foods. I estimated that about three hundred people passed through the kitchen in two hours.

'TWO HOURS! Oh my God. I checked my watch again. I looked around at the others and said, "Okay, Anna, what's everyone laughing at?"

"What do you mean, Geno?"

"Come on, Anna. I can see everyone at the table looking at me, snickering and giggling. What's so funny?"

"Oh, Geno. I'm sorry. But you're just like all Americans. You can't relax. You're always looking at your watch." She repeated this in Italian for the others and they all laughed warmly. I smiled. It was a tension-breaker.

When things quieted I said, "Anna, you say that Americans know how to make money. Right?" She translated this for them. They nodded in agreement with Italian oh-yes sounds.

"Well," I said, "How do you think we make money?" They all looked at me, sensing my seriousness.

"By looking at the watch," I said. I raised my wrist and tapped my index finger on the watch for emphasis. Anna translated. Their faces dropped. It was as if they had just heard the secret of life.

Ahh's and ooh's resounded in the kitchen as if a theater audience had been shown how a magic trick was performed. Each one came over to hug me, thanking me over and over. I could hardly believe it. It embarrassed me. Were they putting me on? But then I realized that they really were simple folk who were even more unsophisticated than I had thought. Their response had been open and honest and completely unaffected. I began to understand that it might be they who knew the secret of life.

Franco drove me back to Naples in his same wild, Italian cowboy, shoot-em-up style. But I hardly noticed. I sat in the backseat, not even looking at my watch. I was thinking of what had happened during the day. Soon we were only a few miles outside of Naples.

POW! went one of the tires. The car careened from one side of the road to other, then back again. I fell against the right door, unable to right myself, and held on trying to lean toward the middle. Franco struggled to get control, but the rear end fishtailed when he applied the brakes too hard, and the little car spun full around several times in the middle of the road, finally bumping and stuttering sideways, before tipping up one side and bouncing down again on its four wheels, coming to a dead stop.

We weren't hurt. Franco sat there behind the wheel and swore—first at the car, then at the tire, then at Anna and me, then at God, the road, the heat, and finally, I assumed, the goat he had hit back in Sorrento.

We got out of the car. He bent down to look at the left front wheel and what remained of the blown tire. Twisted remnants wrapped around the wheel rim, emitted the pungent acrid odor of burned rubber. More cursing followed as Franco dropkicked at the tire with the form that would have done justice to a soccer player's tie-breaking penalty shot. I walked to the back of the Fiat to get the spare out of the trunk.

Franco shook his head balefully from side to side and shrugged. "No, Geno," he said, indicating there was no spare. Together we then pushed the car off the road onto the shoulder. Franco took out a cigarette, lit up, puffed away as if accepting our fate, and turned toward the sea to enjoy the view.

"Excuse me. Franco. *Scusee?*" I said pointing at my watch. "The ship. Barco. Ship. Boat." Franco just looked at me. He gestured toward Naples with one arm, palm up, smiled ironically, shrugged his shoulders, and waved at the boat with his other hand, a gesture that I took to mean, 'What can we do? Good bye boat.'

"No, no, Franco. Ship. I must go quick. Pronto," I said in a sweat.

"Ah, Geno...sorry, sorry." Franco shook his head and shrugged toward the car as if to say, 'Nothing I can do about it now. Look at my car.' He pointed at the wheel. He had given up the fight. I recovered the packages I was bringing to the ship out of the back seat. I set them down on the shoulder of the road, looked at my watch again. I had lost a precious half hour. I held out my thumb to hitch a ride.

Seeing this, Franco, understanding my intent, dramatically held up his hand, a reminder that he was in charge. Stepping out into the middle of the road, he waved with the officious grandeur of a *poliziotto* directing traffic, crossing his arms back and forth at the on-coming vehicles heading north toward Naples. Pretty brave, I thought. When a car finally stopped, Franco went over to the driver, pointed to me, then to Naples. The driver shook his head no. Franco gave him one of his personalized, special finger salutes and a ready curse, both of which the driver returned in kind before driving away.

After ten minutes Franco managed to flag down another car. The driver wore what appeared to be a black cap like a military hat with a red medallion just above the beak. They talked. They laughed. They talked some more. They gestured. Finally, Franco pointed toward me. More talk. The driver nodded. "Quanto, quanto?" Franco asked him.

"Cinquante septe mille lire," the driver said. He would take me in his taxi the rest of the way for "fifty-seven thousand lire". He said this in English and repeated the number for me.

"Fifty-seven thousand lire?" *How can I pay that...there goes my job.* Then I started to figure. At 1800 lire to a dollar, that would be… ah…just a minute…about thirty-one dollars. "Yes," I said. "Okay. Okay. Thirty-one dollars. Let's go."

After Franco helped me load the packages into the taxi, I shook his hand warmly. "Thank you, Franco. Thank you. *Grazie. Grazie.*" In return, Franco hugged and kissed me hard on both cheeks, and said something that sounded like it meant "hurry, hurry." I pressed a ten-dollar bill into Franco's hand, at which he smiled a huge smile and waved goodbye. The race was on. I could only hope.

"You know Teddy?" said the driver after a few minutes.

"No," I said, assuming he meant Teddy Kennedy.

"Oh," said the driver. "My name is-a Pietro. What's yours?"

"Gene….Geno"

"Ah, Geno…that's-a nice. My brother is-a name Geno. He live in United States, too. What part U.S. you from?"

"Near New York."

"Ahh, my brother is-a live in-a Brook-a-lyn. You know Brook-a-lyn?"

"Sure", I said, trying not to be chatty, so he would sense my urgency.

"I love-a-Brook-a-lyn. I love United States. God bless-a you."

"Thank you. *Grazie* Could you please hurry. I have to make it back to my ship."

"We make. Notta to worry. What-a time?"

"The ship sails at six. I'm supposed to be onboard no later than 5:30 PM." I checked my watch. It was already 5:15.

"Hmm," the driver said. He pushed down hard on the accelerator and the taxi lurched ahead.

I watched as we came into Naples onto a six-lane main artery, three of which headed into the center of the city. A truck loaded with metal pipes sped past us on our left in the middle lane. Suddenly it veered to the right, cutting in front of us, and careened violently into a side street on the right. Clangity bangity, bang went piping all over the street, bouncing every which-way, as the taxi swerved to the left to avoid them. Screeeeeech, went the police car's brakes behind us, followed by a loud thud as it whumped the rear of our cab, just as metal pipes smacked into our front end.

The taxi driver had done a good job of avoiding a serious pile up. But a pipe post had wedged into our right front wheel and jammed the steering. The *poliziotti* strutted out of their car, assessed the situation and talked to the taxi driver. Another police car soon arrived, its siren blaring. Pietro was very calm, considering the circumstances. He explained he was cut off and that he was urgently "trying to get Geno to the American ship" which was sailing in just few minutes. Traffic was stopped in both directions. Horns were honking. The two *poliziotti* in the second police car then motioned to me to get in. Paying the taxi driver, I grabbed my packages and plopped them onto the back seat of the police car. Off we raced with its whoop, whoop siren blaring. The flashing blue strobe light on top of the *machina della polizia* warned all Neapolitans along the way that this was serious police business. I held tight to the back of the driver's seat as we maneuvered in and out of traffic with intrepid skill and determination.

We were close now. It was two minutes before six. As the police car approached the port, I heard the ship's deep horn, blaring like a giant tuba, sounding its ominous announcement of imminent departure. *Shit.* The police car pulled up to the gate at the pier entrance. It was closed. No one was there. The driver blared the siren, leaned on the horn until two stevedores and a security guard came out of a shack and swung the gates open. Whereupon the police car dashed down the pier toward the ship, squealing to an abrupt stop at the crew gangway, which had been pulled halfway up. The lines of the ship had not yet been cast off.

Too late. I didn't make it. And so close. Both *poliziotti* jumped out of the car and yelled up to the deckhands to lower the gangway back down. Shouting ensued. The ship's horn blasted again. Heatedly, the two *poliziotti* repeated their orders. The port pilot, seeing the scene from out on the fly bridge of the ship, called down to the deckhands, and after some commotion the gangway was reset in place. As my uniformed friends helped me with my packages, one said to me in very clear English, "Tell-a Teddy...please notta to be President. He coulda be shot like his-a two brothers."

The D.C. crowd, all six of them, watching the bizarre scene from A-Deck, cheered as I stepped on board carrying several bulky bundles wrapped in newspapers and tied with twine, all of which elicited good natured laughter from them. I smiled but couldn't laugh with them.

"Please, don't anyone say anything," I said. "Come with me to my cabin." They followed, helping me with the packages. Once there, I unwrapped each bundle slowly, carefully covering the bed with delicious surprises. The bundles contained extraordinarily delicious fruits, homemade cheeses, pastries, desserts, breads, cookies, candies and treats that the girls had stayed up at night for weeks making for my visit. Two bottles of homemade red table wine promised instant happiness.

I told them the story of my day and about my remarkable relatives, how generous and kind they were, how they had treated me with such respect, like a cherished celebrity, and so had honored my grandfather. I added that I would never, ever, deny them or my heritage again. When I recounted my wild trip trying to get back to the ship, no one laughed. They listened, drank the wine and sampled all the foods with gusto.

"Welcome back, Gene," said Ned. "But in view of what you've just told us, I think you owe us an apology."

"I do?"

"You put your relatives down. Called them peasants. That kind of cranked us up, Genie Boy. Made us sound like a bunch of snobs, and we were only agreeing with you."

"Ned, I apologize. I'm really sorry." I knew he was right. I had jumped to conclusions. I was lucky, and not for the first time in my life, that in this case I'd done what my mother had asked me to do.

"We thought you weren't going to make it back in time once they started to pull the gangway. That's cutting it pretty close," he said. "But what a grand entrance," he added lightheartedly. "We're sure glad to see you."

"Thanks. I can't believe I'm here."

That night in the Empire Lounge, on Sunset Deck, the atmosphere was warm and friendly with guests sharing experiences of their day-in-Naples. We were playing light cocktail music, show tunes, easy-listening stuff, background music. Shortly after my friends arrived, along with the rest of the formally dressed after-dinner crowd, I picked up my Selmer alto sax, turned up the microphone a bit, and made a special dedication. "Ladies and Gentlemen...a toast to Italy," then I played the most soulful saxophone rendition of "O Sole Mio" I could muster. In looking back on the scene, this may have seemed hammy and sentimental. But something had changed in me that day. People stopped talking. They listened, sensing an unknown message. Word had gotten around about my being escorted back to the ship by police, but most of the passengers didn't know why.

When I finished, the crowded room of guests applauded warmly. Young Trisha made her way across the floor to the bandstand and hugged me. *Umm. How sweet.*

Bob LaPlante caught my eye and nodded his wise worldly approval. Ken Duca shook my hand. Sometimes he was a moody guy, especially when he drank—but he was a musical genius. "I hear you, man," he said.

Many weeks later, back in Bridgeport, seated in his favorite old cushioned wicker chair on the front porch, my grandfather wept when I presented him with a small jar of black dirt. Memories of his boyhood home, a home he left over seventy-five years before, nearly overwhelmed him. "Thank-a you; thank you, Genie," he said over and over again sobbing. "You-a gooda boy."

No longer the grumpy grandfather of my youth, he listened and nodded when told about the trip and how everyone had treated me with such respect, and how, thinking I was her brother, Emilana had called me Antonio. He looked into the distance as I spoke, his eyes full of yesterdays. And when I described the luncheon feast, he said in a weak voice, almost a whisper, "Ahh, it was-a-like Chrisymoos for them."

And for me, too. He died two years later at ninety-nine.

*

Well, you reported that story essentially correct. But why not start at the beginning?

(Just wanted to see if you were paying attention. Okay, here we go.)

**

One

ROOTS

It didn't seem so at the time, but a case could have been made that ours was a musical family, quantifiably at least. At nine years old I began taking clarinet lessons—more instruments were added later. Barbara, my younger sister, was a piano student, and Duane, my older brother, played accordion and trumpet. My mother was a professional pianist.

"Grampa," came to America from Italy around 1890 at the age of twenty. He played accordion and mandolin, a beautifully handcrafted instrument, which he made himself. Whenever he ensconced himself in his upstairs kitchen chair to enjoy an hour or two of daily 'practice,' the term *self-taught* took on new meaning.

He saw no reason to change his 'Columbus Method' when searching for the right note: *find it and land on it*. This was difficult to for us. Three of us were taking lessons and practicing, more or less seriously, and my mother was a music teacher. For my grandfather, however, accuracy was the least important requirement for his own participatory enjoyment. His hit-or-miss approach never seemed to affect his personal satisfaction quotient. He lived by the maxim 'The act of doing is its own reward.'

If Grampa overheard a bit of our practicing, he would announce mistakes with a grimace. "Dats-a wrong-a note," as if he were the duly recognized authority on the subject of accuracy. His own playing, exempt from self-criticism, was atrocious. I knew it. So did the rest of the family.

My father, however, though not a musician, was a self-appointed critic. He didn't listen to our practicing, more likely overheard it once in a while reading the newspapers. But when he did, he sensed when our playing wasn't right, though he didn't say what was wrong. You could always tell by the way he winced when he heard obviously wrong notes—'clinkers,' he called them.

Even though music wasn't his passion—more likely it was the Brooklyn Dodgers—his overt reaction to clinkers was his way of letting us know he was aware of what was going on in the crazy household around him. This was particularly evident whenever my grandfather plowed through music in the kitchen of his upstairs flat at night or on Sunday mornings. The results of this ritual were particularly painful for my father.

The sounds of persistently fractured music—wrong notes, little regard for consistent tempi, left-out beats, added beats, a chaotic collage of clinkers—wafted inexorably downstairs into the ears of the unprotected. "Geez. Is he deaf or what?" my father would call out to us. Tolerance and patience did not come easily to him.

Often when I practiced my clarinet, I would set up my music stand in the kitchen so my mother could listen—mistakes, squeaks and all—as she prepared a meal. For a son there is nothing like maternal attention and approval. And because my mother was a musician, I appreciated the audience all the more.

I hated practicing, but she always encouraged me. One day in particular, when, after just twenty minutes she saw I was ready to give up, she said it was okay to stop. We sat down at the kitchen table. First she explained that if a person wanted nice looking teeth he had to brush them every day, even though it wasn't fun to do. And to learn a musical instrument well, he had to practice every day, even if he didn't want to. There was no short cut. "No progress without practice," she said. Another patch of family dogma.

She went on to relate how it was when she was a little girl learning to play the piano. She said her father, her first teacher, was very tough on her. One day she practiced longer than ever before. That night she couldn't wait for him to get home from his barbershop so she could tell him of her first-time accomplishment.

"Poppa, guess what?" she said proudly. "Today I practiced four hours."

"Hmm. You should-a practice a-five," he said.

She wanted to cry. But she didn't. She said it only made her try harder. When I told her I thought that was pretty mean, she said, "No, Grampa wasn't mean. He was just trying to teach me the only way he knew how. If it hadn't been for him, I never would have become a musician. It takes discipline to stay focused on learning music. He just made me stronger."

Still, he sounded crude to me. But I could see that criticizing him was something my mother just would not tolerate. So as I got older I dropped my duty-like attempts to inform her of Grampa's rude ways, something she most likely knew better than I anyway.

She said that when she was thirteen, her father decided it was time for her to be a professional and took her to the neighborhood theater to play piano for the silent movies. He would walk with her the five blocks to the Parkway Theater, a small movie house across the street from his barbershop—he knew the manager and gave him haircuts. The kids called it the Garlic Hall, most likely in reference to the elegant flavoring apparently used generously in the diets of many of its patrons. He would leave her at the door and come back after the film was over. Upon returning, each night he'd collect her money, and give her a quarter each week, which she was expected to save.

When she had accumulated a dollar, he took her downtown to the bank—they always walked to 'save the streetcar fare' – where she deposited her money in a savings account. She told me she hated the bank because she could never spend her money — not even a nickel for ice cream or for anything else, as other kids in the neighborhood did.

When he took her to the movie house that first time, she said, "But Poppa, what will I play?"

"Justa play whatta you wand when you watch-a da picht," he said, and he left her there to figure it out.

So every night she sat in the pit, looking up at the movies, making up music as she watched the stories unfold, playing slow, sad pieces when the movie was sad, and peppy selections when it was happy or when there was action.

She told me that one night there was a very sad scene in which a pretty little girl was dying of pneumonia, breathing weakly in her bed, her dog and family gathered 'round her. The actors in the film were crying melodramatically. People in the movie house were crying also. Even my mother was crying. She didn't know what to play but had to think quickly. Then she remembered a tune she had heard somewhere. And although she didn't know the words or the title, she played it because of its tender melody. When my grandfather came to pick her up later, the manager, clearly displeased, told him she had played "The End of a Perfect Day," and the audience knew it.

Even though Grampa didn't quite understand, he knew it wasn't good. Cuffing my mother's head, he said, "Whatsa matta you, Marguerite?"

When my mother grew up, she was a well-known bandleader in New England during the depression years of the '30s—Marge Hull and her Melody Boys—ten men and my mother. Whenever she told me how well the musicians in her band played, I wondered what it would be like to play in a band.

My sister Barbara and I took dancing lessons every week. Tap and ballroom. We became quite accomplished, and most every weekend we performed our routines at clubs, halls and theaters. My mother accompanied us on the piano. Our act was billed as "Little Fred Astaire and Ginger Rogers," and was and paid five dollars for each performance — my start in professional show business.

Years before our dance-act days, when my sister and I were much younger, a tall, heavy-set young woman, a mother's helper named Irma, used to take care of us at home whenever 'Marge' was away traveling with the band. My father was out of work most of the time, so he'd usually travel with her. We didn't like Irma. She was mean and 'hollered' at us, and she spoke with a heavy accent. She was Hungarian, I believe. However, at that age I really couldn't tell for sure. Suffice it to say that she was foreign, and I could see by her face she wasn't Chinese. Anyway, she developed a habit of slapping my little sister's hand if she wet her pants.

"How are my little sweethearts?' my mother asked one day when she came home from a one-week tour. I must have been about four. I remember she always kissed the top of our heads then picked us up and held us close.

"Mommie," two-and-a-half-year-old Barbara said with a pout, "nurse spank hand much." And she turned up her reddened palms for my mother to see.

It wasn't long after that my mother gave up her band, and we never saw Irma again.

That's when my mother began teaching piano and accordion at Harry Hawley's Studio in Bridgeport. She had so many pupils that eventually she established her own studio. Before long it became the biggest in Bridgeport. My mother was always trying to do things bigger, and it often irritated my father. "Why the hell do you have to have your own studio anyway?" he'd say. "It's always something." He honored the status quo like a true Republican.

My guess is my mother would have been quite famous if she had kept on being a bandleader. She had the drive, energy and vision. But then she wouldn't have been home with us. Obviously, being a good mother was more important to her than anything else. It was a good thing, too, because we missed her terribly when she was away.

It can be difficult to give up something you love for someone you love. But I doubt my mother ever gave it a second thought, even if that something was music.

It would take me a long time to learn that kind of love.

*

Sounds like a noisy house. So far, so good. But remember, I'm watching you.

(Don't worry. You can trust me.)

**

Two

AT THE LYRIC

It's February cold. Depression cold. But no one in the long line is grumbling. In fact, the mood is high-spirited, buzzing, festive, carefree. Waiting with his mother and father, the ten-year old boy wonders about "the surprise." What is it?

He watches the group of boisterous young adults in line clapping hands rhythmically as a short, scruffy, dark-haired man starts to dance on the sidewalk doing some kind of free-form jitterbugging the boy has never seen before.

He tugs at his mother's coat. She is a petite, pretty woman, with brown hair, a good figure. She dresses with flare, to say the least, as befits her image of herself. Today she's wearing a long, bright red, spring cloth coat, even though it's cold; black rubber galoshes cover her high heels. A squirrel boa is draped around her neck. On her lapel a large grand piano rhinestone pin glistens. She sports a black, broad-brimmed Easter hat highlighted by a white faux gardenia. Usually avoiding conventional dress-of-the-season, any season, she knows she's different and always manages to look it. She's supposed to, she thinks. After all, aren't former entertainers always in show business, even after they've left it?

"What's he doing, Mom?" the boy asks. "I never learned any steps like that."

The crowd is noisy. His mother doesn't hear him. She's watching too.

The man is wearing a shabby, heavy brown overcoat with a large tweed cap pulled over his ears. The coat is too long, almost touching his shoes. He bends and swoops like a big bird, brushing against the slush-stuccoed sidewalk when he does. An unlit cigarette dangles from his lips. It falls. Before his parents can stop him, the boy dashes out and picks it up. He holds it up to the man. The man waves him off. The father takes it and throws it away.

More people join in, clapping louder and louder, standing back to make a large circle on the sidewalk. The man is twisting and jumping about wildly. His face reddens; his dark eyebrows seem to touch each other in effort. He grunts intermittently, as the crowd encourages him. "Yeah, yeah. Go Crackers, go!" The father reaches out and with one arm partly shields his son. The man slips, falls down on all fours but quickly rolls over onto his back, kicks his legs high up into the air, wriggling them wildly. It's like he's being electrocuted, the boy thinks, just like in the movies.

When he finishes, the man jumps up and bows to the crowd. Everyone cheers. The boy doesn't understand.

The sky is threatening snow again, a typical Connecticut winter day, damp and gray. But for the boy there is nothing typical about this Sunday afternoon. For one thing, he's wearing his good plaid mackinaw coat over his best Sunday pants and sweater. Why did his mother tell him to dress up? He usually has to do that only for Church.

"Aw Mom, do I have to?" he had said. "Just to see a movie?"

"Do what Mommy tells you, Honey. It's a surprise."

And now there's this guy dancing all wild like. What's going on?

"Why was that man dancing like that?" the boy asks, as everyone resumes a place in line. The episode is a refreshing divertissement for all, an impromptu moment that captures the crowd's attention, just the thing to warm them up on a frigid afternoon. "He looked like he was crazy."

"Wasn't it fun?" she says with a calm and poised expression. " I think he's just excited about coming to see Benny Goodman."

"Who's Benny Goodman?"

"That's the surprise! He's a famous musician, one of the best in the world. And he plays clarinet, just like you."

"Is that why everybody's here? Not just for a movie?"

"Uh huh. Daddy and I thought you'd like to see his stage show with us. Benny Goodman is the 'King of Swing' and he's never come to Bridgeport before. It's a big day today. He has a wonderful band."

"You mean a band like you had when I was little?" the boy says.

"Oh, much better than that. Wait till you hear it."

The boy wonders what it will sound like. He has never heard a live big band before. He's small with a wiry build and expressive blue eyes that do not miss much. His brown, bushy hair wants to go in many different directions. His mother has put Pomade on it. Pomade hair gel is the hair dressing of choice for men and boys in the 1930's and 40's. At least it is in Bridgeport. It smells fruity. His mother doesn't put much on him, just enough to keep the straggly ends in place. It makes his hair shine. 0

"How long are we going to stand in line," he asks. "It's cold."

"We're almost there, Sweetheart," his mother says, reassuring him. She rearranges the scarf around his neck, snugs it up, pulls his hat closer to his ears, and pats his head.

"It won't be long now."

"Do we have to do this today?" the boy asks her. "I'd rather go ice skating at Seaside Park Pond."

"You'll love it, " she says. "Be patient."

He kicks at some snow. "Mom," he says, "why does Duane say I'm a dreamer? I'm not, am I?"

"Your brother is only kidding. Don't pay any attention to him."

But the ten-year old knows what his older brother says is true. Sometimes he does go to an imaginary world. For instance, right in the middle of tying his shoes when getting dressed for school, he'll stop and stare off at something without focusing. But it doesn't seem like dreaming to him; he's just thinking and wondering about stuff.

"Hey daydreamer, I'm not waiting for you," his older brother will say, and leaves for school without him.

These are Depression years. Like most other areas, Bridgeport, a blue collar, industrial city in southern Connecticut, is hard hit. For millions of people it is a nation with little. Unemployment, big bands and movies are the most important subjects discussed. Movie theaters are jammed. Dance halls are like palaces, and music of the 'Big Bands' captivates the nation.

On an entertainment scale of one to ten, today's attraction at the *Lyric Theatre* is a solid ten, a not-to-be-missed event. And all Bridgeport seems to know it. The Theatre's shows are a sell-out.

Since getting a clarinet for his ninth birthday, the boy has been having a lesson every week and practices regularly. His mother has found an excellent instructor for him, a musician who used to play clarinet and saxophone in her band, and who tells her he thinks the boy has talent.

But the boy isn't thinking about music right now. He's still wondering about the strange dancing he has seen the odd-looking man doing. It wasn't at all like the tap or the jitterbug steps he learned in his dancing lessons with his sister.

Gradually working their way forward with the line, they are now about fifty feet from the Lyric's box office. The boy notices the marquee's white lights chasing one another relentlessly around the edges and tries to follow them with his eyes to see where they start. But there's no beginning and no end. He looks at the big black letters on the white background and reads aloud, "On Stage—Benny Goodman and His Orchestra with Helen Forrest." Underneath, in smaller type, he reads, *"The Grapes of Wrath* with Henry Fonda. "

Benny Goodman and His Orchestra will play five sold-out stage shows this day in a theater that holds thirty-eight hundred people. The Lyric's policy is to play a movie alternating with a live big band stage show.

Finally, they reach the box office at fifteen minutes before two o'clock. The boy watches his father pay for the expensive tickets.

"That'll be sixty-five cents for each adult and thirty cents for the child," says the woman behind the glass.

The boy doesn't see any other kids in line. Maybe it's a show for grownups, he thinks. He feels special, proud that his parents have brought him, even though he'd still rather be ice-skating. He hopes seeing the band will be worth it. But he doesn't think so.

They push along into the lobby with the hurrying crowd. Almost smothered, he looks down and sees the floor is white and black marble squares. It looks like a big checkerboard to him. Above people's shoulders he can make out the tops of posters on the walls that say "Coming Attractions."

Everyone bunches together at a doorway where ushers are taking tickets. People are calling out to one other, joking and laughing as they wait to have their tickets ripped in half. Once through the bottleneck, they funnel out into a spacious, fancy inner lobby with a high ceiling. It has thick gray and red carpeting, the kind you sink into a little when you walk. Big golden-framed mirrors hang from the red cloth-covered walls. What a fancy place, he thinks.

Most people do not stop at the candy and snack counters. Instead they surge forward directly into the auditorium, rushing down the aisles to get seats close to the stage. There is no reserved seating. By this time the main orchestra section is already half full. The boy and his parents find three seats together fairly close to the stage and settle in.

The boy looks up at the ceiling and all around. Never has he seen such a beautiful theater. It's the biggest one he has been in. As a matter of fact, it's really the biggest place he has ever been in, bigger than his school and way bigger than Sacred Heart Church. This has two large balconies. There are sculptures of *bare people* all around and a mammoth red curtain with tassels hanging on it in front of the stage. A huge, lighted, crystal chandelier is suspended from the middle of the ceiling.

He's been to other theaters, like the Parkway and the Cameo, but they're small compared to the Lyric. He wonders if that's because the Lyric is downtown? He notices that many of the young ladies are dressed in pretty dresses—but not the same as his mom's. She looks better. But they look beautiful too. He stares at them. They don't notice him. Some men wear ties. So does his father. He still doesn't see any other kids.

"Dad, how high is this ceiling?" he asks

"Pretty high, I guess," his father says.

"But how high?"

"Oh, I don't know. What difference does it make?" He turns away to put his coat under the seat in front of him. The boy

GENE HULL

looks up and ponders the ceiling height. *Bet you'd get killed if you fell from there.*

The boy's father is a short, thin man, with dark curly hair. He has a strong, chiseled face. He dabbles as an actor and subs as a sort of stage electrician or 'something like that' in the Park City Community Theater. He used to be in the Naval Reserve. Now he's an airplane mechanic, whenever there's work at the factory. But when he comes home from work he mostly falls asleep on the couch. The boy thinks his father would rather be an actor or in the movies. He's smart and knows lots of things, even if he does get impatient easily. He knows the good actors and the good movies, and he says movies are "corny" that he doesn't like. The boy wonders why; they seem okay to him.

His mother always says, "Yes, Dear," and "No, Dear," when she and his father have a discussion. His father acts like the boss of the family. But the boy knows his mother is actually the leader, the one who has ideas and is always thinking of things.

Maybe his father resents this. The boy has thought about this before. He figures this might have something to do with his father getting 'mad at nothing', usually when his mother has an idea to go somewhere or do something different. Like, "Let's go downtown and see the lights tonight."

He's glad his father isn't upset today. *It must be awful to be mad so much.*

It's two o'clock. The theatre house lights dim. It's time for "Coming Attractions," after which comes the "Movietone News of the Day." The news is mostly about the War in Europe.

"Dad. Dad!" the boy says. "Why are there airplanes? And soldiers? And who's on the stretchers?"

"It's a war," his father says.

"But why is there a war?"

"Because of Hitler."

"Who's he?"

"A dictator."

"What's a dictator?"

"Shush," says the father, "the movie's going to start."

The boy watches "The Grapes of Wrath" and fidgets. He's restless. His feet are cold. He doesn't understand the movie. It's too long and slow. But he can see that his father likes it from the way he seems to be concentrating, staring at the screen, mouthing words with the actors, now smiling, now frowning.

"Dad, I thought we're going to see Benny Goodman today," he whispers loudly.

"We are," his father says, "right after the movie."

"Why do they call it "The Grapes of Wrath"?

"That's a long story."

"I don't see any grapes."

"That's because there are no grapes."

"Why not?"

"Shush."

"Why don't they have a cowboy movie instead?"

"Hush," his mother says. "Leave your father alone."

At the end of the movie the main curtain lowers again. The house lights come on. The chandelier lights up. Immediately, people start whistling and stomping their feet, chanting, "We want Benny. We want Benny."

"That's for Benny Goodman, right Mom?"

"Uh huh. They can't wait. Isn't this exciting?" she says.

The boy nods. But so far he's not as excited as he was when the man in the long coat was dancing outside on the sidewalk. Now he's not sure what to expect. He hopes he won't fall asleep, like he almost did during the movie. A drum rolls. He hears music coming from behind the curtain, and the audience begins to cheer, as if they know what's coming.

The house lights dim, and the main curtain opens. But wait. There's a second curtain, a filmy one, all bathed in a bank of colorful lights. It looks purple and silver and shimmery.

"That's a scrim," his mother says, pointing to the stage. He can see the band through the curtain, but not clearly, and he can hear the music. He waits. *When will the scrim open? Why is the band behind it? Maybe it doesn't open.*

Finally the scrim curtain rises slowly, teasing the audience; and as it does, the sound of the band gets louder. Finally the whole Benny Goodman Orchestra is revealed, with Benny himself standing in front in a dark blue suit. He's wearing horn-rimmed glasses, *like Father Healy wears.* White spotlights shine on him and he waves… a little.

The crowd cheers and whoops. He turns around, faces the band, makes some kind of hand signal. The trumpets and trombones stand up, and the sound they make smacks the boy full in the face with a musical force that pushes him back in his seat. It's a fusillade of brass notes, a wall of sound. The boy has no idea music can be so powerful.

Benny smiles at the audience, not a big broad smile, just a small one, then picks up his clarinet and joins in with the band. He solos at the microphone. His clarinet sounds alive to the boy, like a person talking fast and making jokes and almost telling a story. *A clarinet can sound like that?* Behind the solo, trombones slide and punctuate riffs, getting louder and louder as Benny plays higher and higher, until a point where the whole band is producing rich sounding chords that keep getting bigger and broader. It sounds like they're going to explode, the boy thinks.

Then, as Benny climbs to the highest clarinet note the boy has ever heard, the band hits a final gigantic chord and holds it while the drummer plays freely all around the drum set until the final cutoff. The crowd screams in euphoric delight.

A song called "King Porter Stomp" comes next, and the brass attacks again. *It's like they're biting at the air.* The boy feels a strange thrill moving up through his legs—like the time Gertie Collins kissed him at her party. Yeah! ONLY THIS IS WAY MORE. The sax section stands up and dazzles him. *How can they play so fast? And so together?* The drummer's beat seems to electrify the whole band.

More players come down in front. They go to the microphone and play jazz solos, like Mr. Goodman does. They're not reading music either—*making it up as they play!* First one trumpet player solos. Then another. Then the tenor sax player. Then Benny again. The audience applauds. So does the boy.

By this time people are dancing in the aisles. The ushers let them. The boy doesn't know where to look next. He's smiling so much his face hurts. He loves the way clusters of lights color the stage with blues and golds and reds and purples. He squeezes his mother's hand. She smiles at him. She seems to know it is the most amazing thing he has ever seen or heard.

Suddenly Mr. Crackers jumps up on one side of the stage, still in his old overcoat and hat, and starts doing flips and wriggles on the floor.

"Mom, Dad, it's him!"

The man whips off his coat and throws it out into the audience. They cheer. The boy looks wide-eyed at his mom. A spotlight swings over onto Crackers. Benny Goodman moves to the other side of the stage and watches Crackers dance. He tucks his clarinet under his arm and starts clapping his hands in time to the music. The crowd loves it and whistles and yells, "Go, Crackers, go!" The boy joins in. After the number is over, ushers escort Crackers off the stage. The crowd cheers him. He waves at everybody. For the rest of his life he'll be remembered in Bridgeport as the guy who danced on stage when Benny Goodman came to town.

Without warning the music seems to fade to a distant undertone in the boy's head, as if his ears are plugged, and he sees himself on stage, out in front of the band, playing wild notes on his clarinet. The spotlight is on him. People are clapping in rhythm. The men in the band cheer him. "Go, Gene, go!" He sees his family from the stage. They're smiling. They're so proud of him. He feels wonderful!

Slowly the live music floods back into his ears, and he's back in his seat. The stage lighting and the incredible pulse of the music is almost too much for him. He holds his mother's hand so tightly that a thousand words couldn't tell her any better how he feels.

"Oh Mom, thank you, " is all he can manage to whisper.

"Someday you'll be up there, she says clearly. And he knows she believes it.

"What are you telling him that stuff for," his father growls.

She doesn't answer. Instead she gives the boy's hand a secret little squeeze.

As the band plays its closing theme "Goodbye", Benny steps down from the stage, comes up the aisle to the row where the boy is sitting. He gestures to the boy. The boy can't believe it. "Go on, " his mother says." He leaves his seat, goes to the end of the row. Benny shakes his hand, asks his name, and brings him up on stage. The crowd applauds.

Benny announces, "I've been watching this young lad all through the show. He hasn't missed a note we played." (Applause) "Are you a musician, by any chance"?

How did he know? Did my mother send a note up to the stage during the show?

"Yes, I play the clarinet. "

"Are you good?"

"Well, my mother thinks so. I practice a lot. I can play "SWEET SUE" pretty good.

Benny hands the boy a clarinet. The boy is bewildered. *What'll I do?*

"Ladies and Gentlemen, Gene is a musician and is going to play "SWEET SUE" with us. Hit it, guys."

Again the crowd cheers. The band intros, the boy plays the melody. Benny jams around him. The crowd loves it. They play another chorus. The band stands up at the end and applauds the little boy. Benny hires him on the spot for the next show. His mother and father stand up and cheer. His picture is on the front page of the paper the next day. *A star is born.*

*

Ahem!

(Oh, right. It isn't quite like that.)

As the band plays its closing theme, "Goodbye," the boy listens until the very last note. The curtain lowers. The house lights go up full and the Lyric starts to empty. People are happy, singing, and bouncing along up the aisles. Band notes swirl in the boy's head.

Darkness has replaced daylight by the time he and his parents leave the lobby. It's snowing. They cross Main Street and wait at the corner for the bus that will take them home to Black Rock Avenue at the South End. The bus ride costs ten cents each. But for twenty-five cents you can get three tokens. The boy knows that his father will get the tokens.

Head-lighted cars and buses splatter freezing slush along Main Street in both directions, while the family waits. The boy looks at the long line of people on the other side of the street. It continues around the corner. He gazes up at the marquee. It's brighter now in the twilight and transforms the falling snow into twinkling colors. The words blur out of focus, as once again the boy is 'on stage,' playing in Benny Goodman's Band. *The crowd applauds him. He's famous. He smiles graciously. He bows.*

"Genie, for God sakes, wake up! Watch your step!" his father says, as the boy half stumbles up the two, high steps onto the bus. "Pay attention to what you're doing. Tsk, tsk."

"Oh, right. Sorry, Dad."

Seated on a cold leather bus seat, the boy stares out the window into the quiet snowy night, not focusing, losing himself in the future.

**

That's better.

Three

MAYBE SOMEDAY

I think my mother knew when she presented me with a clarinet for my ninth birthday that someday she would find a way to buy a saxophone for me. From the way I had reacted when my parents brought me to see Benny Goodman — hardly able to contain myself — she must have sensed the possibility of a music career in my future, which I'm sure was fine with her. To be a professional reed musician in a big band she knew it would be necessary to play saxophone as well as clarinet.

Of course at the time I had no idea she was planning this. I don't think my father did either, because if he had, he would have said no, like he did with most 'schemes' my mother would 'cook up'. However, his negativity never seemed to deter her. She'd just go ahead and set about doing whatever it was she had in mind, then tell him about it after the fact. Or sometimes he'd just find out for himself. She was an irrepressible doer who believed it was easier to get forgiveness than permission. This saxophone story is a case in point.

On my twelfth birthday—my 'sax birthday' I call it—we were sitting at the kitchen table after supper, my father, mother, brother, sister and I. The dishes hadn't been fully cleared yet, but some of us had already started on the ice cream as the cake was being served. As usual I'd managed to spill ice cream on my shirt. My brother giggled. My sister, embarrassed for me, offered me her wide-open blue eyes in sympathy. My father shook his head with the impatience of one who suffers when witnessing the bumbling of others.

"Sorry, Dad," I said.

"Here, Gene, use this wet dish towel," offered my mother.

Through the open window I could hear the neighborhood kids playing in the street. During Daylight Savings Time, August nights were always the best for long games of street Kick-the-Can or touch football. So after we all sang "Happy Birthday," I said, "Can I go outside now?"

"Not yet," my mother said and proceeded to bring out a big, weird-shaped package covered with sections of different pieces of leftover wrapping paper and tied with red string. She wasn't exactly a natural-born present-wrapper, a detail that never seemed important to her.

"Happy Birthday, honey. This is from Daddy and me."

I tore through the paper and quickly uncovered a gleaming, 'golden' alto saxophone – actually brass. "Wow! It's beautiful. I love it."

"We'll get the case for it later," my mother said. "Just keep it in a pillow case for now. You'll have to be careful."

I was ecstatic. On the other hand, I knew it must have been very expensive. "Mom, where did you get the money for it?"

"Yeah, Marge," my father said. "Where did the money come from? The boy's already got a clarinet. What the hell's he need a saxophone for?"

"I sold a few things," my mother said quietly. "Besides, you know the doctor said playing a larger wind instrument would be good for little Gene's asthma."

"Christ! You and your ideas again. Damn it." He slammed his hand down onto the kitchen table. A dish jumped up, did a flip, and shattered on the yellow, red and gray linoleum floor. Creamed corn left on the plate splashed all over. "You could have told me," and he stormed out of the kitchen.

I watched my mother. She looked down at the broken dish and the splatter-dashed floor, then said quietly, "All right kids, now finish up your desert. You can go out after clean-up."

It was 1941. America was recovering from the long Great Depression. The ominous clouds of war were sweeping closer to our shores. Factories had reopened, gearing up for the country's possible entry into World War II. Prosperity was just around the corner. But to me, completely unaware of the outside world, it seemed that most families in our neighborhood were poor—except maybe for the Sencys. They had emigrated from Hungary many years before and owned a small meat market and grocery store across the street from our house. I think we always owed them money. They extended credit to just about every family on our block. Even though "big fat" Mr. Sency grumped about it, Mrs. Sency always insisted. She was a gentle lady who wore her graying hair in a bun.

"Here, Genie," she'd say softly, as she wrapped the pound of ground beef and five pork chops, my mother had ordered, into two packages of shiny white butcher's paper, tying them with thick, white string. "Tell your mommy I'll put this in the book."

"Thank you, Mrs. Sency."

Albert, their son, had been my best friend, along with Richie Gavlick, since we were five. We played ball in the street all the time, and I couldn't wait to show him my new sax. Later in life he became the most revered biology teacher Stratford

High has ever known, for thirty years exciting young minds with the wonders of dissected frogs, plant phylum and the anatomy of beetles and bugs.

Anyway, back to the birthday supper. I can see why my father was upset. Money was always in short supply. And again, my mother had not consulted with him.

"I'm sorry, Mom," I said, after he had left. "Is it okay to keep the sax?"

"Of course," she said, "You know how Daddy is sometimes."

"Can I join a band now?" I said. "That's what I really want to do."

"I know, sweetheart. But you'll have to have lessons first."

I had a private lesson every week. I didn't like to practice, but I did every day. After several months Johnny Kryzanki invited me to join his band. Once a week, after supper, I took the Bridgeport East Main Street bus over to Pulaski Street for a rehearsal at Johnny's house. The neighborhood was heavily populated with first and second generation immigrant families—Polish, Russian, Lithuanian, Slovak, Hungarian.

Johnny's flat was on the second floor of a yellow three story house, above Wasco's vegetable market, which stayed open at night. Every time I walked up Johnny's hallway stairs, the initial scents of fresh fruits and vegetables gradually gave way to heavy odors of pirogues and the cooked cabbage Mrs. Krazanski usually made for dinner Wednesday nights. The pungent smells became more overpowering as I got closer to the top. When I knocked at the door, and Johnny let me in, I'd be almost overcome with a cabbage attack. To this day I avoid cooked cabbage.

Neighbors jammed into the living room and dining room to listen to our rehearsals. We made many mistakes. They didn't seem to mind; it was a neighborhood happening. Two other kids also played saxophone in the band. They were older than I was, but I played a bit better, so Johnny made me 'first sax.'

Besides Johnny, there was another trumpet player, a pudgy looking Jewish kid named Ralphy. Shy and polite, he always wore a clean, white, ironed shirt and a tie. His playing wasn't strong, but then again he didn't make many mistakes.

Danny was the drummer. He perspired profusely when he played, as I recall — even in wintertime. Cabbage wasn't the only smell permeating the rehearsal area. I usually smelled like cabbage and sweat when I got home.

Larry Plessinger played piano. The Kryzankis had an old brown upright, topped with a blue vase of fake flowers. Red-haired Larry was short, like I was, so he had to put a pillow on the stool to reach the reach the keys and pedals. He wore glasses and had big ears. He played very well, and he was smart too— he knew how to transpose at sight. I liked him. (Larry grew up to be an important research engineer at General Electric.)

We all read music and took lessons, including Danny, even though he was just the drummer. Johnny played lead trumpet pretty loud. It hurt my ears when I sat in front of him, but it was better than sitting next to 'Danny the Stinker.' Johnny was the oldest, sixteen. He had big husky shoulders and a crew cut — we called them zip haircuts back then.

My brother also had a zip. In fact, that became his nickname. At the time I remember thinking Johnny must not brush his teeth very much, because they looked yellow. My mom always told me to brush my teeth every time I went out, even before I'd play touch football in the street. It was a thing with her.

"Movie Stars all have perfect white teeth," she'd say to me. That gave me something to think about. Maybe when I grew up I'd be a movie star. Well, why not? I thought about it sometimes when I went to the movies and saw all those pretty actresses. It seemed like a good idea. So I brushed my teeth often and with great gusto, until one day the school's visiting dental hygienist told me I was brushing too hard and would injure my gums.

From what I could see, Johnny had no chance of ever being in the movies when he grew up.

Johnny's father helped us when we practiced—he played upright bass with a polka band. A large friendly man, always smiling, joking, talking, it seemed to me his expansive stomach was held up by a tightly cinched belt, the end of which dangled loosely. His shoes were the biggest I had ever seen, probably size fourteen. When we rehearsed he'd sit in a chair along side us and stomp his foot in time with the music. Sometimes the thumping was louder than the drums.

By the second rehearsal we started playing stock orchestrations, music that Johnny's father had bought at Gilman's Music store. We always played from written music, because none of us knew how to improvise.

I still carried my sax around in the pillowcase. No one seemed to notice; at least they never asked me about it. My mother said we'd get a case as soon as we could afford it.

One of the things I liked about rehearsals at Johnny's house was that everyone applauded after we played even half a song without stopping. It made me feel special. And at the end of a rehearsal, his mom always had pastries and Nehi sodas for us. What a nice lady.

Following rehearsals, Mr. Krazanki drove Ralphy and me in his old four-door Chevy to our corners on the other side of town. I'd take the music home with me so I could practice it. We were pretty serious about being a good band. But of course we didn't sound anything like Benny Goodman. At the time I figured that would take a while, maybe a year or so. Nothing seems impossible at that age.

After six months I was playing in two bands, Johnny's and Stanley Wokowski's. Later, I started my own band. We all played in each other's bands. Today you'd call them 'garage bands.' but not many folks had garages in those days. Whoever had the music could be the leader. I saved up money and bought my own stock arrangements.

My band had four saxes, three trumpets and Freddie Parisi played trombone. He didn't play very well, but he did have a trombone, and every once in a while he landed on the right note, and it sounded good. My friend Larry was the piano player. Of the three bands, mine was the biggest.

Soon I was playing weddings most Saturday afternoons, either with my band or someone else's. Sometimes we'd get hired to play for a dance on a Saturday night at the White Eagles Polish Hall. We'd make a dollar or a dollar and a quarter each. Often we'd play for just for tips—it didn't matter. To me I was almost a professional, getting paid, earning money playing my sax. Ah, the sheer euphoria of it.

The blissful bubble burst when one night the White Eagles people complained that they couldn't dance to our music and refused to pay us. It never occurred to me that grown-ups would do that. They seemed mean to me and I felt helpless. I remember being insulted when they criticized our music. But more than likely we sounded rather out of tune and probably missed more than a beat or two here and there. In any case, I realized then that life wasn't always fair, so I decided to get even by getting better. And I resolved that when I did, if I played there again, I'd ask them to pay us first, before we started to play.

Johnny's band broke up suddenly. One morning Mrs. Krazanski – carrying a full laundry basket—fell coming down the long flight of stairs, tumbling all the way to the bottom. She must have been there all day. Johnny found her when he came home from school. She died a couple of days later. There were no more rehearsals at Johnny's house after that.

My band improved rapidly. I was always looking for kids who could play better. We rehearsed as often as I could get everyone together.

GENE HULL

Everybody said we sounded great. In fact we got so good that we started rehearsing in the back yard so more neighbors could come and hear us. Soon the yard was packed.

The next week my father started charging ten cents admission, but still the people came. It was magic. Our music was just what the neighborhood needed. People danced and had a great time. After a few months we had so much money my father bought a new car, an Oldsmobile, I think. It was our first car. The newspaper sent a photographer and did a big write-up on us. Local dignitaries started coming to hear us. The Mayor asked us to play a concert at City Hall and invited school kids from all over the city to come hear us. We were famous already. It didn't take as long as I'd thought.

*

Uh huh. And two and two are five. I know what really happened. And that's not it. And how about some of those names?

(Tsk. Tsk. Okay. So I changed some of the names for privacy's sake. Picky, picky. But you're right, the story did end a little differently.)

Everyone said we sounded great. Of course that was the opinion of the neighbors — always excellent and impartial judges of talent. But I began to see that becoming as good as Benny Goodman might not be so easy. Being really good at music was a lot different than just playing for fun. I realized that becoming an accomplished musician might take a lot longer than I thought. But when I got there, I guessed then I'd be famous.

After all, my mother said I'd be famous someday. It was sort of taken for granted.

She was always saying things like, "Someday when you're famous," this; or "someday when you're famous," that. So I kept on practicing. And I brushed my teeth every day, too, just in case. Fame might come either way.

I couldn't wait to grow up.

It takes forever when you're thirteen, almost fourteen.

**

Four

THE RITZ

World War II was in the news every day. Big Bands didn't come to the Lyric Theatre anymore. If you wanted to see name bands during the summer you went to Pleasure Beach Ballroom on Sunday nights. In wintertime it was the Ritz Ballroom.

Everyone loved the Ritz. It was the social center, the place for young adults to hear great music and meet each other. My mother said I was too young to go there. "It isn't a place for kids."

By the time I was fourteen and a half, I figured I was old enough. I'd been playing sax for almost three years and thought I knew everything about it. So I proposed that I could learn more quickly by listening to the famous bands live at the Ritz.

"It's an older crowd," she said, "and there's drinking downstairs. Besides, you'd have to take the bus, and you'd be out late. There's school the next day."

I explained that was no problem for me. "I don't drink, I'll take the bus. And I'll be home early. Please can I go?"

In the interest of my having a positive learning experience, I believe, she gave in. "All right, but make sure your homework's done first. And be careful. Call me when you get there."

That wasn't quite all there was to it. I had a plan that I didn't tell her about. I was taking my saxophone with me.

Most every Sunday night thereafter that's just what I did. The bus that took me to the Ritz was always jammed. Each week I'd board at Park and Fairfield with my sax protected in its pillowcase. I still hadn't gotten a real case for it, but that didn't matter. If my plan worked, I'd soon be able to afford one. I sat up in the front of the bus right behind the driver, cradling the weird-shaped pillowcase, pretending to look out the window at something important. I could tell that other people were looking at me and snickering. I made believe I didn't notice them.

Admission was $1.10 to see the biggest name bands and 75 cents for the not-so-famous ones. Movies were 26 cents in those days, and gas was 15 cents a gallon. The older girl at the ticket booth always said, "Good evening, Gene," giving me my ticket, smiling down at me though the glass, leaning forward so I could hear her through the half-circled hole at the bottom. She had dark hair and a very pretty face. I liked the fact she knew my name, but I wished she wouldn't have been so obvious in greeting me like a little kid with all the adults standing in line. It just attracted attention to my pillowcase and me.

Every time I entered the ballroom the sound of the band's brass section would hit me full in the chest and make my rib cage vibrate. I loved the feeling. The manager kept an eye on me. My mother must have called him. Once inside, my ritual was to walk around the ballroom first, then call my mother and tell her I was fine (the pay phone cost a nickel). Then I'd find a place right next to the bandstand, opposite the entrance, and sit there with my sax on my lap, listening to the music, waiting for the "announcement." After staying there for two hours, until intermission, I'd take the 10:05 P.M. bus home.

To me the Ritz was a magical place. I could get next to the world-famous big bands and hear their sounds in the closest ring of audience. I liked the jazz-oriented big bands best, especially those of Stan Kenton, Boyd Rayburn, Claude Thornhill, Gene Krupa, Charlie Barnet, Benny Goodman, Harry James, and Woody Herman – he was my favorite. Once a month great 'colored bands' like Jimmie Lunceford, Count Basie or Duke Ellington appeared. I never went to see them. My mother said it would be better not to. I never asked why.

The Ritz was a long, white, wood-frame building. It had a low ceiling, a sunken dance floor and a capacity of over 3,000 people. That was if people were dancing. But most fans stood, packed in a huge semi-circle in front of the band, absorbing the excitement, limiting the dancing to the extreme ends of the dance floor. One night the crowd actually reached over 4,000 for Guy Lombardo – not my style of band, too 'schmaltzy.'

From the outside the Ritz didn't look like much. But inside it was elegant, with it's long, polished hardwood dance floor and glittering chandeliers. Blue and red carpeting covered the elevated promenade that surrounded the sunken dance floor. A white balustered fence with a varnished oak railing on top encompassed much of the dancing area.

Above the floor, accordion-pleated red drapes gathered from the sidewalls, swooping up to the middle of the ceiling and gathered around the chandeliers. The drapes reminded me of the inside of the coffin I saw at my grandmother's wake in our house when I was little boy. I thought it was beautiful. Some things leave a lasting impression—I can't recall my grandmother's face, but I can remember the coffin's interior.

The Red velvet cushioned benches, which lined the walls, were occupied by dancers or voyeurs who sat between dances and rested, flirted, or just watched the other people.

Downstairs was a noisy bar with a separate soft drink service area and a jukebox. I checked it out but never spent much time there. I was at the Ritz to listen and absorb. Besides, everyone there was much older than I, and that was kind of intimidating.

The elevated bandstand was situated along one side in the middle of the ballroom. However, you could walk completely around the ballroom along the promenade, even behind the bandstand, so it was possible to look over the musicians' shoulders and see what music they were playing. Local musicians always gathered behind the bandstand and smoked cigarettes and talked boisterously, like they knew everything, and greeted each other as if they were just as important as the famous musicians up on the bandstand.

I would sit right along side the bandstand each week, waiting, holding my sax, hoping. This was my plan: someday, it could be tonight, there would be an announcement on the public address system. An important voice would say, "Your attention, ladies and gentlemen. Attention, please. The band's lead alto saxophone player has been taken ill. Is there an alto saxophone player in the house?"

I'd be right there. I'd take my sax out of the pillowcase and be ready to play for the famous bandleader who needed me. I'd save the day. I'd be discovered, soon to be famous. This was a real possibility to me. People get sick all the time. So each time I went to the Ritz, I'd say to myself, *Tonight may be the night. I'm ready.* The possibility of the glorious fame of it all gave me more incentive to practice and improve each week.

Faithfully, month after month, I kept the Sunday night vigil. By this time everyone who worked at the Ritz knew me, and people on the bus recognized me. I knew it was just a

GENE HULL

question of time before the important announcement would come. And I would be up on the bandstand playing my sax with all those wonderful professional musicians.

But no sax player ever took ill, at least not ill enough to stop playing. I listened carefully each Sunday night, but the announcement never came. I even told the manager that I was 'available' and had 'my horn with me.' "Thank you, Gene," he said. "I'll keep that in mind." He must have been amused.

Eventually, after several months of bus-riding to the Ritz almost every winter Sunday night, I realized that my plan, albeit conceived with the optimistic logic of a dreamer, wasn't going to be. Nothing was going to happen. I wasn't going to be discovered this way. My mother had the wisdom to let me find that out for myself.

Soon after, I got my long-awaited case. It could carry both the sax and my clarinet. With it came a new outlook. I thought of myself as a budding professional, not a kid anymore. After all, I had a case now. No more childish dreams about being discovered. I decided not to waste a moment, hunker down and prepare seriously for the 'big time'.

I dove into personal practice with renewed vigor. By the time I went to college, my daily practice sessions were three to four hours. I was determined to be ready when the right opportunity came along. My sight-reading skills sharpened till I could gobble up written notes like breakfast cereal. I formed the official University of Notre Dame dance band—a big band called *The Lettermen*. We played for many functions, proms, and events, like the Saturday night Victory Dances during football season. In those days Notre Dame didn't lose football games very often, so we had plenty of work.

For the next four years I was able cover much of my tuition costs with earnings from the band. I was also the concert band saxophone soloist and first clarinetist in the marching band.

Following graduation I returned to Bridgeport and formed several working combos.

One wintry Sunday night, about ten years after my 'Ritz daze,' I was at home watching television with my wife and our three young children. We had finished dinner and were cozy in the living room of our rented apartment watching the Ed Sullivan Show. Senor Wences had just finished his hilarious talking-thumb act. I remember the kids holding up thumbs against their fist moving their thumb knuckles up and down like a lower lip, imitating Wences: 'Tsawright? 'Tsawright. 'Tsawright? 'Tsawright." We were all laughing. Ed introduced the next act, "Topo Gigio." Circus music brought him on.

The phone rang. It was for me. Ray Colonari, still the manager of the Ritz Ballroom, knew I was a professional musician, since my bands now frequently played in local clubs and for dances and parties at the Ritz. He remembered me from the days when I was a polite little kid going to the Ritz on Sunday nights with my sax and a dream in a pillowcase.

"Gene," Ray said, "How are you? You play sax, right?"

"Sure I do, Ray."

"You play baritone sax, too?"

"Yes, I do. Why? What's up?"

"Claude Thornhill's band is playing here tonight."

"I know. And it's a fine band. Heard him years ago."

The bells were ringing. Could this be the night? Was it possible? After all these years was I finally getting the call to play with a name band at the Ritz? But on bari sax, not on alto? So what. It didn't matter. It was the Ritz. And it was a name band. This was my chance.

"It's happening!" I called out to my wife, putting my hand over the phone.

"Huh? What's happening?"

Ray continued. "Something's happened here at the Ritz tonight."

"Uh huh," I said. I couldn't wait. I could hardly believe it. Oh, thank you, God.

"You know Gerry Mulligan, the baritone sax man with the band?"

"Yeah, sure. He's famous. A fine player. One of the best."

"Well there's a problem. Maybe you can help us out tonight. Jerry and the lead alto player just got into some kind of an argument with a drunk when they were setting up. The alto player took a wild sock on the lips. He can't play. And Jerry's horn got banged up."

"Sorry to hear that, Ray."

"Can you come out here and take the lead alto player's place tonight and bring your bari for Gerry to play? It might be a big break for you."

I don't remember driving out there, but I was there in twenty minutes. My heart was pounding as I took my horn from its case and stroked it a few times. Dry-mouthed, I swallowed several times until I could whistle. I sat down in the lead alto chair without being introduced to Thornhill or the guys in the band. A nod and smile was the proper protocol required. Musicians shaking hands on a bandstand made customers and venue operators uneasy. 'Is this the real band or a pick-up group?'

During the fourth tune there was an alto solo and I nailed it beautifully. It just felt right. Pent up feelings, accrued in years of struggling, let go with exuberance. Thornhill seemed amazed. On both sides of me I heard. "All right. Too much! You play!" Frankly, I played the best I ever had. Before my next solo Thornhill introduced me to the crowd as a fine "guest artist" from Bridgeport. They gathered around the bandstand and cheered each time I played any kind of a solo during the rest of the night.

Thornhill asked me to join his band for its current tour until his regular alto player was well. At last I had broken through. I was on my way. This was the opportunity I had hoped for. The feeling was unbelievable. Excitement. Pride. Anticipation. Gratefulness. It's amazing how sometimes your dreams can come true, and when you least expect them to happen.

*

Oh yes, speaking of dreams, that was an interesting ending to the story. I'm sure you're going to change it. Right?

(Okay, okay. So Ray actually, said…)

"You know Gerry Mulligan, the baritone sax man with the band?"

"Yeah sure. He's famous. One of the best."

"Gerry's horn isn't working right — some key is broken. And I was wondering… could we borrow your bari tonight?"

Suddenly I deflated and got depressed. No, that doesn't come close to what I felt. I was crushed. Just when it looked as if the moment might finally be and was dangling right in front of me, poof, it was gone. I suppose it was one of life's little ironies. Everybody gets teased once in a while. It was just my turn. Get over it, I said to myself; you're not a kid anymore, even if you are a dreamer.

"Sure, Ray. I'll bring it right over."

I felt like kicking something. I couldn't believe this was happening. It was actually funny, when you think about it. But I was too numb to laugh.

"Ha," I managed to say as I hung up the phone.

GENE HULL

"What so funny?" my wife said.

"Oh, nothing. I've got to go out to the Ritz and let someone borrow my horn. I'll be back in a little while."

I drove to the Ritz in my eight-year old blue Plymouth, the bari resting in its case on the back seat. I gave the horn to Ray and never let on how I really felt. I was too proud. I sat along side the band in my old familiar spot, habit, I guess, and listened to the great Gerry Mulligan play my baritone sax brilliantly. Time flashed back to the many nights years before, when I was a kid. I remembered the excitement and anticipation and how hopeful I was.

Now as I gazed around the ballroom, I saw that I was older than many of the patrons. Local musicians weren't enclaved behind the bandstand anymore. People no longer gathered *en masse* in front of the band as in former years, cheering and applauding each individual soloist. They were dancing. The charged atmosphere was gone. The era of big band mass hysteria was in flux, changing to what, I didn't know. But I didn't like it.

After a few tunes, I couldn't listen any more. I got up, found Ray and said, "I'll pick up the horn tomorrow, Ray."

"Fine," he said, "I'll have it right here. And thanks a lot, Gene. You saved the day. I won't forget it."

"Sure. Glad to help. Anytime."

I went outside and moped in front of the Ballroom. I stood there, kind of blurred out. It was snowy and cold. The green and white bus came by and stopped. People got off. I got on. It was brightly lit and almost empty. The floor was wet where snow had been tracked and melted. We bumped and bounced our way back to town. I thought about all the times I went to the Ritz as a kid with my horn. I thought about the music and the fine band I had heard that night, and the telephone call, and my family, and playing my sax, and never playing in a name band…or even being a movie star.

Twenty minutes later I got off at my stop and walked home.

"You okay?" my wife said.

"Sure." Then I told her what happened.

"Well, it just wasn't meant to be this time."

"Yeah, I guess so."

The next morning I went outside to get in my car. It wasn't there. I shook my head, a little puzzled. Then I remembered it was still parked out at the Ritz.

So was my saxophone.

**

Five

ME AND MY SHADOW

"**No, damn it!** What do you think you're doing? That's the way I play. Nobody plays the way I play. Only Ted Lewis plays that way!" I wouldn't forget those words.

At twenty-five I accepted my first traveling job with a name celebrity as lead alto saxophonist with the Ted Lewis Orchestra. It wasn't a jazz band, true, but it was a chance to get experience. And though the pay wasn't great, the work was steady. I was anxious to do well and was optimistic. What a wake-up call it turned out to be.

A lean man of medium height in his late 60's, Ted Lewis had a craggy, ruddy face, seriously interrupted by a prominent nose. His wavy white hair, always carefully groomed, swooped back perfectly with just the right flair. He was a striking man who commanded attention whenever he spoke in his booming theatrical voice—one of those people who knows he's important and makes sure everyone else knows it too, even if he's saying, "Please pass the butter." Every utterance for him was a platform to impress.

Billed as the 'Tragedian of Song,' Lewis presented a stage and floorshow revue with dancers, singers, a novelty act—Irving playing "Hot Canary" on a miniature violin—and a ten-piece band. The show featured Ted playing his clarinet and telling stories. These were mostly nostalgic tales of "the old days, when life was simple and people were polite, and bread was five cents a loaf." (Or was it when life was polite and people were simple?) They were romantic tales of yesteryear, all recounted by Ted in grand style, every verb emphasized, every adjective milked with shameless disregard for subtlety of any sort. And yet somehow it worked, mesmerizing his fans.

Ted's theme song was "When My Baby Smiles at Me." But more famously, he was the one who originally created and performed the classic dramatization of the tune "Me and My Shadow," the highlight of his show. It was artfully presented. Putting down the clarinet, he would pick up a walking cane and stroll back and forth across the stage, gesturing like a Shakespearean thespian, like an old time vaudevillian—like himself—all the while singing the title song with the controlled fragility of a much older man. *"Me and my shadow, strolling down the avenue..."*

The stage would be dark except for a spotlight on Ted, accoutered as usual in tux and tails and weathered old collapsible top hat. But a second spotlight, one of lesser lumens, would capture the movements of another person on stage, Ted's shadow, dressed the same as Ted, except totally in black. The shadow mimicked every one of Ted's gestures, every step, every movement.

Stopping mid-stage, with a grand flourish Ted would tuck the cane under one arm and light a cigarette, letting the perfect smoke rings undulate up through the bluish light, morphing into hoops then vanishing in the darkness. He'd pause, as if savoring the moment, while the violinist carried the plaintive melody from one measure to the next.

Sensing the right moment, Ted would resume his stroll and sing the rest of the song, doffing his battered top hat to the audience with the aplomb of a gallant Maurice Chevalier. His shadow would do the same.

Just before leaving the stage, Ted would pause at the wings, gaze out into the spotlight and invoke the familiar wistful phrase everyone was waiting for: *"Is everybody happy?"*

The act was total theater. And primarily because of it, Ted had become a show business legend. Later in the show, some of the band members (trombone, trumpet and clarinet) would come down front and join 'Ted and his clarinet' in recreating a jam session from "Rector's Restaurant in 1910 back in Old New York," as Ted would announce it. Johnny (I never knew his last name) played the jazz clarinet solo in this number.

During the second month of the tour, on Johnny's first night off — I don't recall his last name — I was told I was to play the solo in his place. I was called to Ted's dressing room before the show. A private audience with the star? It felt strange, particularly since he had never spoken directly to me before. This must be important. Maybe he likes my work. Maybe he's going to give me a raise? There the maestro was, seated at a small dressing table in his boxer shorts and black patent leather dress shoes, garters and socks—with his top hat on—patting pancake makeup onto his face with a small, damp sponge. At regular intervals, he would take off the hat, check the mirror, dab a little more makeup here and there and put the hat back on at a jaunty angle.

"Yes, Mr. Lewis?" I said from the doorway.

"Let me hear the solo you're going to play in the show tonight," he said without looking around.

"You mean you want to hear my improvisation?"

"Yes, yes. Right now. Play it for me."

"But then it wouldn't be an improvisation."

"Damn it, I want to hear it now!"

"Okay, sure." I hadn't thought about what I was going to play on stage. But it occurred to me then, that since I had been listening to Ted play his clarinet for several weeks now and had a pretty good idea of his style, he might be flattered if I imitated him. So I launched into my 'improvised' solo, playing a rather coherent collection of his favorite stylized licks. Not bad at all, I thought.

"No, damn it!" he boomed in his W.C. Fields voice, whirling around on the bench. "What do you think you're doing? That's the way *I* play. Nobody plays the way *I* play. Only *Ted Lewis* plays that way!"

"Okay, Okay. I'll play something different."

"You better! And let me hear it right now."

I played some standard old Dixieland kind of phrases. Nothing too hip. Nothing creative or inspired. I was just sort of kidding. But he approved. I couldn't believe it.

"That's better. That's more like it. That's what I want to hear tonight. That's what my audience wants."

But later, in the show, after my 'backstage audition.' I played a stunning new improvised solo, nothing like what Lewis expected. Lewis went ballistic. He didn't know what to do. His face reddened. I thought he was going to throw me off the stage. But the crowed cheered madly when I finished. Lewis stopped the show and introduced me to the audience. More thunderous applause. That night after the show he gave me a raise and asked me to play my own creative solo every night for the rest of the tour.

*

My, my, what a fertile imagination. A raise? From Lewis?
No way.

(Well, that's the way it happens in the movies.
And you're right. There was no raise.)

Later in the show, after my backstage 'audition,' I repeated the same solo Lewis had approved, note for note as close as I could, in what was supposed to have been an authentic impromptu jazz jam session. I resented having to do it. I was young enough to be idealistic about that sort of thing. But in the context of the show it was appropriate, and Lewis had been right. I still didn't like it.

Much later I realized that the Ted Lewis experience had taught me the meaning of a maxim well worth remembering. In show business people pay to be entertained, not to be 'educated' by someone trying to elevate their tastes.

They don't teach you that in music school.

**

Six

IS EVERYBODY HAPPY?

Weeks had gone by since the Pittsburgh night when I had played the 'fake' clarinet solo for Ted Lewis. We had moved on and were playing an extended engagement in Memphis.

On this sultry summer night I was feeling particularly restless. The separation from family was getting to me. If anything was bothering me, it usually surfaced in this kind of weather. There was something about the heavy, static atmosphere that seeped into hidden irritations—like, why am I here anyway? I questioned whether the road would bring me closer to my goals.

That night, after we finished playing our two shows at the Peabody Hotel, Lewis announced to the band and cast that we were invited to a private party in his hotel suite in an hour or so. I was in my antsy mode and not too anxious to attend. I hadn't forgotten the way he had demanded that I play my jazz solo for him in his dressing room. I had felt insulted then and was still smarting like adolescent.

So instead of going to the party, I went out, walked to an all-night diner and had breakfast. Surprisingly, the stroll in the foggy dampness of the night refreshed me. Nature's nightly thermostatic adjustments were well under way, as another warm Memphis evening yielded to the inevitable nocturnal invasion of Mississippi mist. Intermittent fog rolled off the broad river, billowing into downtown, colliding with hours-old sidewalk heat, wilting forgotten flags, cooling sycamores and oaks, moistening car windows till they dripped. It was cooler, somehow cleaner. No cigarette smoke. No noise. No people.

I gave more thought to attending Lewis' gathering. It occurred to me that even he if was overbearing, I was taking myself too seriously. I resolved to redirect my energies and not let my personal antipathy toward him keep me from getting on with making a living as a musician.

Once back at the hotel, I decided I'd better go up to his suite and put in an appearance. Maybe he's taking attendance. You never know. No sense in not going. One of the other musicians let me in.

The gathering seemed quiet enough. Just a little easy talk here and there. People stood around holding drinks, a few guys from the band, some others I didn't recognize. Soft music from a record player filled the void between casual conversation and the clinking of cocktail glasses. Someone handed me a glass of Chablis. I sipped a sip; it was bitter. I preferred beer. Or maybe a Scotch? I stood there holding the glass and looked around. The lights were subdued, but I noticed that several people seemed to be focused on something of interest on the far side of the spacious, floral-carpeted room. Seated on a large couch, two partially clad giggly young women and one young man, wearing nothing but boxer shorts, were getting better acquainted.

Another young woman, this one in black panties, emerged barefoot from a bedroom with a black ostrich boa draped around her neck. Other extraneous accoutrements were lacking, but her personal attributes were extremely generous. Sashaying over to the couch, she extended both ends of the feathered serpent from her outstretched arms, stepped gracefully up onto the coffee table, and commenced performing slow, sensuous hip gyrations in sync with the music.

Someone turned up the stereo until the sound of "Harlem Nocturne" bounced off the walls. The couch tomatoes, and carrot, proceeded to remove each other's remaining garments, while the boa-draped one slithered around an invisible pole.

Amazed, completely surprised, embarrassed, yet curious, I could feel my face getting warmer. Then I noticed the impresario himself, clad in tux and silk smoking jacket, seated across the room watching intently as the action steamed ahead. When the boa-clad young woman began undulating with increasing intensity, he bellowed out to one of the musicians, "Get the camera! Get the camera!"

I was captivated… until he spoke. Hearing him, commanding and bullying, triggered some sort of unpleasant activity in my nervous system. I began churning inside. I didn't know why. I knew that in his long career this man was regarded as a class act. He had been in feature films and played the most sophisticated supper clubs, theaters, and show rooms around the world. I'm sure he deserved his fame. So even though I didn't like him, I tried to be understanding. After all, who was I to judge? One's choice of recreational activity is a personal matter, and has little bearing on professional ability.

Nevertheless, this particular activity seemed to be outside the kind of behavior I could be associated with, even if it was a private party and he was famous. I wasn't a prude or particularly fragile, but I was young and not road-seasoned. So reluctantly, but resolutely, I left the party and considered leaving the band and going home, when I could afford to.

Perhaps the years spent in a Catholic prep school and university had left some indelible impressions on me. Anyway, I like to think so. However, it had to be more than that. These were adults, productive, successful, talented, in a business that traditionally is open-minded and free-spirited. The scene was really no big deal. So what was really bothering me? Why did I react with such black-and-white judgmentalism? Was I really that embarrassed? Or did I fancy myself an example-setting martyr for the other musicians, as if by staying at the party, I would be approving the scene? Possibly. How naïve. But my subconscious motivation was Lewis' voice and manner. To me it was dismissive, insensitive and belittling. It made me see red.

Sure, he was the boss. But why did his attitude and voice bother me so much? Was I being overly sensitive? Maybe. Whatever the reason, before the tour ended, even though I was working with some talented people, I decided not to renew my contract for another tour, if asked to do so.

Years later, a realization invaded my brain like a truth serum. I began to understand why I had been so agitated. Somewhere in Lewis' voice was the demanding tone my father used when I, as a kid, would trip or drop a glass or break something accidentally, or misplace his hammer, or forget a chore. Often I'd hear him yell on and on at my mother, too, indulging in out-of-control tantrums. I cringed from it whenever he unloaded with one of his red-faced tirades. And when he yelled at me, I did nothing except apologize. I knew he loved me and cared for me, and didn't intend to hurt. He just couldn't help it. I also knew it wasn't good for me.

On the other hand, my mother was always telling me how wonderful I was, and how I was going to be a big success when I grew up, and that I was thoughtful and kind and talented. No doubt her constant reinforcement helped to give me confidence. Perhaps it also led me to seek others' approval too much.

I guess I needed to replenish my supply of self-esteem. More than anything this probably keyed my desire to achieve. While I'm sure my father's anger dented me, most likely it also impelled me to be somebody.

Strange as it may seem, Lewis' voice reminded me not only of my father's darker moods, but also my grandfather. He'd scold me for something foolish I had done when I was little: like when I moved my head the wrong way while he was giving me a haircut, or fell asleep with the radio on some nights. It was just his way. I know my occasional dreaminess irritated him. He never thought I'd amount to anything. I can still hear him hollering at me, even when I was a young man of twenty, because I didn't begin painting the walls of his barber shop the way he wanted it done.

I didn't like the bullying then, and I didn't like it now. I had observed that sometimes people with bully power, whether they be bandleaders, or bankers, secretaries or CEOs, schoolteachers or kids, subconsciously regard subordinates with less than personal respect. They focus on what they perceive as a person's deficiencies. In my view, the relationship doesn't change. The habit usually worsens. So early on, I resolved to distance myself forever, if I had a choice, from anyone who belittled me, talked down to me, bullied me, or made me feel less than a man. Ted Lewis qualified as an offender in my book.

On tour with Lewis, I had conflicting emotions. I wanted to be successful and I needed the experience and the work. Yet I recognized the old bully-and-intimidate syndrome only too well.

So it was ghostly echoes that had spooked me. And I knew they would only get louder, unless I got out of there.

In an effort to solve the problem, the next night I sat down to talk with Lewis after our show. Hearing how offended I was, he understood and apologized, said it would not happen again. The rest of the tour was delightful.

Lewis apologized? Oh really?

(It would have been nice if he did. I like happy endings.)

Too bad. The facts, please.

So it was ghostly echoes that had spooked me. And I knew that they would only get louder, unless I got out of there.

Lewis and I never reached an understanding. I'd like to think that leaving the band when the tour was over was an honorable decision, based solely on integrity and strength of character.

But actually, I didn't like the music either.

**

Seven

THE AUDITION

"When are you leaving?" she said.

How do you tell your wife that you're desperate? That you're quitting your job at the department store? That you're leaving home for the second time in a little over a year? That you're taking another traveling job, this time with a name band?

You're twenty-six and life is passing you by.

You're a young father with four kids now. You have responsibilities... and dreams. What do you say to them? Daddy wants to play his saxophone? Daddy can't stand working in the store? Daddy hated working in the factory? Daddy hated being a census taker? Daddy can't make enough money playing weddings and bar mitzvahs to support his family? Daddy is dying inside? Daddy feels like a failure? Daddy doesn't love you as much as he does music? Of course not.

What do you tell your family who loves you and only wants you to be with them? How did it all ever get to this point? When the Ted Lewis tour was over, I returned home and worked a succession of day jobs, anything to keep from going on the road again, even if the road meant steady work, especially with the kind of bands that played commercial cornball stuff. I had had enough of that. While it still was music and served a purpose for older people, it was watered down, had no edge, no swing, and it wouldn't bring me closer to attaining professional goals. So if I had a choice, I decided to avoid playing it.

I continued the practice-hours regimen on sax, clarinet and flute, taking lessons in New York, playing every kind of gig I could find in the Connecticut area and working part-time day jobs. But it wasn't enough to pay the bills. I had to find a better way to support my family without traveling. There just wasn't enough full time work in music to sustain us. So, like so many young artists-in-waiting who do not find employment expressing their artistic needs, I sought work outside of music.

I took a job in the Junior Executive Training Program at Holland's Department Store in Bridgeport, part of the Allied chain. I started as a part-timer before Christmas, running the 'Lionel Railroad' layout in the toy department. Seeing me there shocked some friends. I was four years out of Notre Dame, where I had been president of my class one year, and I was already a known bandleader in the Bridgeport area. I'm sure hometown people expected bigger things of me than running toy trains in a department store. I did too.

There were some sensitive moments. Dottie, my ex-girlfriend from high school days, whom I hadn't seen in years, was walking past the other side of the toy department one day. She did a double take, recognizing me, but quickly covered her mouth with a gloved hand and turned away, as if concentrating on some nearby store mannequin—a sudden move to keep from meeting my eyes. I couldn't blame her. There I was, wearing a gray and white striped engineer's cap with a red bandana around my neck, tooting on a wooden, three-toned train whistle, trying to attract shoppers to the Lionel train display. It was sort of clownish.

From then on, whenever shoppers recognized me, I'd smile and give them a big wave and call out, "Hi," a maneuver that usually headed off awkward conversations. Usually they'd manage a weak smile, a nod, and a whatever-happened-to-Gene look, before hurrying on. I understood. I was embarrassed, too.

From toy trains, I was promoted full-time to 'Children's Shoes.' And then to 'Ladies' Shoes.' From there to Assistant Shoe Buyer. In a few months, I was promoted to buyer in the basement annex for 'Budget Ladies Coats, Suits, and Dresses.' It seemed I had finally established an economic beachhead. I attended all the training courses and company seminars. I was the up-and-coming young executive-in-training on a fast track. Store management and employees seemed to regard me with deference. Putting on a different hat doesn't change who you are, but it has its place. I never let the job define who I was. I was still a musician.

One day in particular altered the course of my career in retailing. Once each week I'd train into New York City and shop the market for next season's budget fashions. This spring I was looking for ladies fall coats.

It was a Wednesday, about noon, late March, on Seventh Avenue in the Garment District. I splattered through the slush from a late spring snowfall and made my way into a corner drugstore to get warm and have a sandwich and a hot chocolate.

The place was crowded with lunch-hour people, its narrow aisles packed with clutter, displays, bookracks, and cardboard boxes. A maze. Mice must have enjoyed their nights when the store was closed. I could hardly find the way to the lunch counter in back. But when I did, I bumped into my old roommate buddy from the Ted Lewis Band, Al Verst. I hadn't seen him in over a year.

Al played alto sax and was a good man. Handsome, about thirty-five, dark-haired, always smiling, a mellow kind of guy, he was a dead ringer—only shorter—for Tony Martin, the famous singer married to Cyd Charisse. Cyd was a tall, exquisitely statuesque movie-star dancer. When Al and I were on the road together, I used to kid him, as if he actually were Tony Martin, the husband of Cyd.

"So Tony," I'd say, "Do Cyd's legs really start at her armpits?"

"Sure."

"She must like midgets, huh?"

His comeback, in warm Brooklynese, ala Jackie Mason, was always, "So whaddaya think, my hands are small too?"

Al saw me first, just before I reached the lunch counter. "Geeeeennnn. It's so good to see you, man. What a surprise! What are you doing in New York?"

I told him about my new job and about shopping for fall coats for the store, trying to sound like a rock-solid business retailer. Al wasn't wearing a outer coat. I took him for a store employee. "So what's with you? What are you doing here?"

"I'm working, man. I manage the place for my uncle."

"No kidding. You'll own the store someday. Playing any?"

"Naw, not any more. That's history. I'm getting married. The music business is dead. How about you? Still married to Connie?"

"Sure. Four kids now. Two boys, two girls. Beautiful family."

"Still playing your horns?" he asked.

"Weddings and club dates at home, but I'm pretty much out of it now." (I lied.) "I've got a career going in retailing, and I'm home with my family."

"Uh huh. Still practicing and taking lessons with Joe Allard in the City?"

"Oh sure. Something might happen. Maybe a record deal or something."

"Uh huh, I see. You know, I heard that Tex Beneke is in town auditioning for a lead alto player today up at Nola Studios."

"Really? Ah, that's not for me. I'm not interested." (I lied again.) "I'm settled now. I'm a buyer. Besides, even if I wanted to try out, just to see if I could cut it, I don't have my horn with me." I was off the hook.

"You could borrow Joe Allard's horn. Just call him up and tell him about the audition. You're one of his better pupils. He'd let you use it."

"Aw, I don't know… " Slipping gradually into a 'what-if' mode, I started thinking about the possibilities. Opportunity was knocking at an inconvenient time.

"Well if you want to audition," said Al, "the band manager's name is Eddie Matthews. Call Nola's and ask him if they're still looking for a man. What do have to lose?"

"Hmm... I don't know, man. Gotta run, sorry. Al, it was great to see you." We shook heartily. I never saw him again.

With that I turned and retraced the circuitous route back to the front door. I didn't eat lunch. Once out on the sidewalk, I realized that I just couldn't walk away from this. What harm would it do just to see if I could make it? To see if I were good enough to play lead sax in a real name band? What would it matter if I just auditioned? Who would know? I wasn't going anywhere, anyway. But what if…?

I had a serious consultation with myself there on the crowded sidewalk, getting bumped into by people who seemed to know where they're going and were busy trying to get there. I escaped to a pay phone booth on the corner and called Joe. Yes, I could use his sax.

Then I called Nola's and spoke to Eddie Matthews. "Yeah, sure," he said, "If you study with Joe Allard, we want to hear you. Come over in an hour." Momentum was gathering.

Nola's was on the corner of Broadway and 54th Street. It occupied the entire second floor loft of a large building and had several rehearsal rooms of various sizes. The outside studios had floor-to-ceiling windows that could swing open. In summertime, you could stand across the street on Broadway and hear great bands rehearsing at all hours of the day and night. When a famous band was rehearsing, you'd see many people up there sitting and standing along the windowsills inside. A year ago I had gone in with a friend to watch Dizzy Gillespie's big band being rehearsed by Quincy Jones for a State Department Cultural Exchange Tour to the Middle East and Latin America. Extraordinary music. Awesome musicians, way beyond my level.

At precisely two o'clock, I walked into Nola's and immediately got an eerie feeling — as if famous notes were still echoing in the halls. Almost numb, I made my way to the largest rehearsal hall, Studio A. It was the same studio where I had heard Dizzy's band with those great jazz musicians.

Studio A had faded yellow walls and a high ceiling that obscured the dingy paint between its brightly lit florescent lights. Several floor radiators were busy hissing, trying to smother the room's March chill. The Tex Beneke band, thirteen musicians, was set up at one end of the long, rectangular room. *Wow, there they are. And there's Tex himself.* He was standing in front of the band, facing them, listening intently as they played. He wasn't as tall as I thought. I was psyched.

On three sides of the room about thirty wooden folding chairs were set up in a single row. In each chair a nervous looking guy sat facing the band. Different ages. Some dressed in shirt and tie. Some in sweat shirts. A few had beards. A couple sported berets. But each cradled an alto saxophone on his lap waiting to audition. I was wearing a business suit.

As I walked in, one fellow was auditioning, sitting in with the band. I stood by the door and listened. He played a solo. I could tell in an instant I was a much better player.

Apparently the band had been auditioning players for about an hour. They still hadn't found what they were looking for. If they had, they would have stopped auditioning.

"Eddie Matthews? I'm Gene Hull," I said, when the song was over.

"Yeah, the guy from Joe Allard's."

"I guess," I said.

"Good. Get out your horn. We'll hear you next."

Before the others who are waiting? Hum. I blew a few notes, wiggled a few keys, and sat in the vacated audition seat, the lead alto chair, in the center of the sax section. Tex stood right in front of me, facing me.

I was pretty relaxed. I didn't need the job. But sitting there, I realized how much I wanted to show him I could play. In fact, I wanted to show everyone there, and my friends and family, and the people back at the store. Suddenly I wanted everybody in that studio and everywhere to know who I was, that I was a good player, ready for the 'big time'. I wanted the job. I wanted to be the lead alto man with Tex Beneke. The adrenaline kicked in.

He counted off a ballad that had a tricky but beautiful alto solo. I flubbed a note. He stopped the band. "That's an A sharp," he growled, looking down at me.

"Oh, right." I didn't look up.

We played it again. I played it perfectly this time. Tex didn't say anything to me.

"Guys, pull out 'American Patrol.'"

This arrangement featured plenty of ensemble sax section work, with the lead alto right out there in front, charging ahead. It swung. I played it pretty well. Tex strolled over to Matthews and murmured something to him.

"Let's take five, everybody," Matthews announced. They talked more, head to head. I figured that with thirty guys yet to audition, they wouldn't be taking a break yet, unless I was the one they wanted. Immediately I put the horn in its case – yes, I had a case for my own sax at home now, too—and walked out of the studio into the hall. Before Matthews could get to me, I found a phone booth and put in a dime.

"Yes, operator, collect to anyone from Gene Hull. Thank you"

My wife answered.

"Connie, guess what? Tex Beneke is auditioning today in New York. He's looking for a lead alto player for a tour."

Silence.

"Well, just for kicks, I borrowed Joe Allard's horn and auditioned...just wanted to see if I could make it. Ya know?" Still no response from her.

"You there, Con.?"

"Uh huh,"

"Well, I'm sure I've got the job if I want it. But I'm telling them no thanks. No way I'm leaving you and the family and the store job just to play a road gig, name band or no name band. Just thought I'd call and tell you. I'll catch the five o'clock home from Grand Central."

*

How unselfish. Are you sure that's what happened when you called your wife?

(Hmm. Now that I think of it, the conversation went more like this...)

"I borrowed Joe Allard's horn for the audition…just wanted to see if I could make it. Ya know?" Still no response from her.

Matthews was pounding on the phone booth door. "I need to talk to you," he mouthed.

"Just a minute, Con." I opened the door, leaned out, said "Eddie, when does the tour start?"

"Friday."

"You mean the day after tomorrow?"

He nodded.

I shut the door on Eddie. He paced back and forth.

"Connie, sure is crazy around here. I, a…actually, I, I'm sure I've got the job, if I want it."

A long silence. Then, a sigh. "When are you leaving?" she said quietly. Too quietly.

"Two days," I said sheepishly, feeling like a heel. "It's really a career move."

"I know," she said. "Come home."

"Right. I'll get the five o'clock from Grand Central."

I was so excited I could hardly speak.

My wife was crushed. I could hear her disappointment. She realized, I'm sure, that her hopes for my staying with a stable career – like retail management—were again being vanquished by an infrangible force she had come to recognize but felt powerless to resist.

She was a saint.

I wasn't.

You rat.

(Ow.)

**

Eight

SATURDAY NIGHT IN TEXAS

"**R**emember guys, it'll probably be the same tonight as it always is here. So be ready when the time comes." Tex Beneke was standing in front of us with his back to the dancehall audience. It was a few minutes before we were to start playing. Some of the musicians laughed knowingly, apparently not concerned about his remarks.

"What did Tex mean by that?" I said, wide-eyed and innocent, leaning over to Hermie, the veteran saxophonist sitting beside me. Hermie always seemed to know what was going on.

"You'll find out," he said with a wry smile. We searched through our music folders and pulled out the arrangements for the first set.

What did Hermie mean? Why all the mystery? Be ready for what? But because I was new with the band, I didn't ask any more questions.

Saturday night in Longview, Texas, 1956—a year after the Ted Lewis tour—was our stop today. The Brooklyn Dodgers were on their way to winning the World Series. The "New Look" was in, skirts were long again. And I was the lead alto saxophone player with the famous Tex Beneke Orchestra. We were on a spring/summer tour of one-nighters throughout the Midwest and South.

Bandleaders like Beneke, who had built big reputations during the Swing Era's halcyon days, were now touring more and more to "Flyspeck, USA," performing in person for pockets of fans who knew them from their many hit recordings. Since Tex had taken over the Glenn Miller Band at the end of World War II, his music library had many memorable hits, like "In The Mood," "Tuxedo Junction," "Moonlight Serenade," "String of Pearls," "Little Brown Jug," "Kalamazoo," "Serenade In Blue." And here I was, playing in his band.

I was proud to be in the band, but I did have mixed emotions. I was excited and thrilled to be there, of course. Yet I wanted the experience to be worth the decision I had made to leave my family for another tour. I was happy, sad, anxious, hungry to learn, afraid to fail, and all too well aware this was a chance to validate myself as a professional musician, an opportunity I couldn't afford to waste.

Longview, Texas was a town of small farms and a few oil rigs. Post-war urban expansion and commercial development was on its way, but hadn't yet taken hold. Neither had the interstate highway system. With a population of about twenty-five thousand, and a hundred twenty miles east of Dallas, it was still a cowboy town in spirit. You could see cattle being driven by cowpokes on horseback near town, crossing a road here and there.

People generally minded their own business and worked hard in Longview. And, as I would discover later, they played hard too. One place they liked to play hard was in their dance hall.

The Beneke band was booked to play one night at Longview's Longhorn Ranch Dance Hall. It wasn't a ranch, and it wasn't exactly a hall, but rather, almost-a-building structure, half the size of a football field, mostly open sided, situated on a scruffy prairie about five miles from town. The Longhorn's wooden bandstand, a three-foot high, tiered platform, sat on the concrete floor at one end of the hall. The night air probably cooled the place. But when there was no breeze, whew!

We arrived at Longhorn Ranch on our chartered Greyhound bus at 6:00 PM that hot June late afternoon, after an eight-hour, bumpy, 300-mile haul from Tulsa. The bus pulled up behind the building, close to the bandstand back entrance. The first thing I noticed was the strangling heat that reached up from the ground. There wasn't even a patch of a cloud overhead to give temporary relief. Every time I took a deep breath I could feel the heat pouring into me. It was hot—Texas hot, June hot, Saturday night hot, sticky hot, Jack Daniels hot.

Miles of parched land stretched off into the distance, dotted with shrubs that were probably tumbleweeds in the making. I wondered why anyone would want to live out here in this dismal dirtscape.

Since we weren't staying in a hotel that night, but would be traveling on the bus to the next town, right after the dance, we didn't unload our bags, just our instruments, equipment, and the usual shaving cream, tooth brush and razor.

The typical one-nighter bus tour pattern was: travel all day, get to the dancehall, set up, get dressed, play the gig, get back on the bus, travel all night, arrive at the next town early in the day, check-in to a hotel, sleep till late afternoon, set up, play the gig, go back to the hotel, sleep there that night, get up the next morning, get back on the bus and start the process all over again. I adapted to the routine easily. Booking into hotels every other day and spending alternate nights traveling saved money. That was always a plus, because band members paid for their own hotel rooms.

After setting up the music stands, lights, wires, and unpacking the music, Eddie Matthews, who rode with us on the bus wherever we traveled, went about the business of checking the PA system. Eddie took out Tex's gold-plated microphone to begin the sound check and connected it to a cable already in place He did the same with the 'girl singer' mike. A few of us stood around to watch and listen.

"Testing, testing, one, two, three. Check, check. One, two," Eddie said," Check, check, testing, testing." *Etcetera, etcetera, boring.*

I wondered why, just for once, someone didn't say something different during a sound check. Like maybe throw in some Shakespeare, just for laughs.

> *Is this a dagger I see before me,*
> *the handle toward my hand?*

Testing.

Come, let me clutch thee.

One, two, three.

I have thee not, yet I see thee still.

Check.

Art thou not fatal vision
Sensible to feeling as to sight...?

Check. Check. Check.

Oh well, why not?

The younger musicians in the band all agreed the place sounded like a barn. Hell, it was a barn. I wanted it to sound like Carnegie Hall and fully expected that it should. But the musicians who had played here in past years were indifferent. They had more important things on their minds, like finding a pay phone, reading newspapers, catching up on stock market quotes, writing music, practicing and sniffing out the locals.

Two men already had their eyes on the young women who had gathered around to watch the band set up. After all, this was a name band, a sufficient flame for some local moths.

Duke Belmont, the drummer, and Vinny Castellani, one of the trombone players, had struck up a friendly conversation with two lovely young local cowboyettes, pretty as butterflies in their Saturday-night pastel dresses. Seems that Duke had met one of them the previous year when the band had passed through. Knowing the importance of advance planning to enhance possibilities of testosteronian success in the fast-paced, here-today, gone-tomorrow life of a road musician, Duke had called ahead to let her know the band would soon be in town. The man was motivated, always thinking ahead. Seems like every band had at least one dedicated musician like him.

The scene reminded me to call my wife, which I did every other night. The separation was rough on the family. I ran up a hellava phone bill on that tour.

We felt pretty gritty after the long, hot ride. There were no showers, so after set up, we used the sinks in the men's room to wash and shave.

"Hey Hermie," I said, "there's no hot water."

"Welcome to the road, man, " he drolled, as he cruised his electric shaver across his face.

"What was Tex talking about when he said to be ready?" I asked.

"You'll know soon enough."

"Come on, man. What's up? We going to have to march or something?"

"In a manner of speaking, yes," he said.

I really didn't get it. But I didn't want to appear too curious, so I shrugged it off. We ate some sandwiches, had a few cold beers and soft drinks before going back onto the bus, which was air-conditioned, thank God, to change into our uniforms: black tux pants, black patent leather shoes, powder blue dinner jackets with shawl collars, blue cummerbunds, white shirts and matching blue bow ties. Tex was in a midnight blue tux. This was Saturday night in Texas, and Tex was a favorite son, so it was dress-up night.

I felt important wearing the band uniform. Looking back, we were playing the kind of music worthy of getting dressed up for, and the crowd expected it. Of course, times have changed. If a contemporary band went on stage dressed that way today, they'd probably look more like a country club wedding party.

We strolled onto the stand fifteen minutes early to get ready for the first set. I noticed a few sparsely spaced ceiling fans overhead, whirling around lazily, not pushing much air. Two floor fans, set up at the sides of the bandstand, were aimed at us. If they were supposed to keep us cool, somebody was a dreamer, or a salesman.

Finally we were set up, tuned up, and ready to go. It was eight o'clock. But just before we started, a chicken wire curtain, the width of the bandstand, was lowered from the rafters in front of the stage and secured to small hooks in the concrete floor, the bottom angling out a few feet onto the dance floor. It was like we were caged animals for everyone to look at. It turned out to be the other way around.

"Really, Hermie," I said, "that's wild. I never saw that before. What's the chicken wire for?"

"You'll find out," he said, busy making adjustments to his octave key with a tiny screwdriver. Hermie was a man of few words. As usual our first tune would be Tex's signature theme song, "Moonlight Serenade," probably the most recognizable Big Band theme song of the era. It had been Glenn Miller's theme, the first and last tune we played every night.

The band drew a big turnout. After all, it was Saturday night in Longview. The famous Tex Beneke Orchestra had come to town to play all the Glenn Miller hits. No self-respecting citizen could stay away. Everyone showed up, even the mayor.

He introduced us with a big "Ladies and Gentlemen, as your mayor it is my distinct pleasure to present the pride of Texas, Mr. Tex Beneke himself, and his fabulous orchestra!" The crowd cheered like the freshman bleacher section at a college football game.

"Wow," I said, "this is really something, huh, Hermie? Listen to them. They love us already."

"Yeah, sure," said Hermie, nodding casually.

Women in party dresses. Men in chinos and cowboy boots. Some dressed in jeans and short sleeve shirts. Others in fancy western shirts and string ties. More than a few kept their cowboy hats on. Some wore jackets and ties.

Everyone had brought liquor, and everywhere coolers were stashed full of beer. Long tables with black pipe legs lined both sides of the hall, facing in toward the huge dance floor like out-of-bounds markers. Each table, covered with a shiny white paper tablecloth, sported a plastic bucket of ice.

It was "Moonlight Serenade" time. Well over three thousand good citizens of Longview had invaded the dance floor by the second note. No one was shy. No one waited for someone else to start first. They swept *en masse* out onto the concrete like a flood and immediately began dancing. After all, that's why they were there, so why waste time.

The sparkling overhead mirror ball began its slow, glittery rotations right away. No waiting to be introduced as a special effect at some appropriately romantic moment later. Hell, no. Shoot the works right away. The crowd was warmed up and raring to go. The night had started at an energy level usually only reached by the halfway point.

By nine o'clock, the place was rocking like New Years Eve at an Elks Club in Erie. The din became a roar and kept climbing. The booze was flowing. The Good Times were rolling. And boy, was it hot.

After the first forty-minute set, we took a twenty-minute break. Off came our jackets. We were all sweating so much that I wondered if the crowd could smell us. Vinny, the t-bone player, immediately put on a clean shirt and spent the break next to the bandstand chatting up one of the local lovelies he had met before. While the girl was ooing, cooing, giggling and fondling his tie, a couple of big young dudes, really big—I mean, these guys must have been 6'6" at least, wearing Stetsons, boots, and jeans, with tee shirts rolled-up to their shoulders—were moving toward Vinny. As they got closer, I could see them glowering at him with threatening, tough-guy looks that definitely didn't convey brotherly love. Evidently this was their territory and Vinny was poaching.

I also noticed that Duke the Drummer was missing, and so was Miss Pastel Dress Texas-ette number two.

Fortunately, just about then Tex called the musicians back onto the bandstand to start the next set, and the big galoots walked off. I was on stage first, ready to go, since I had a solo coming up and was silently 'wood-shedding' the notes on my horn. As I did, Duke came hustling in through the back door and ran up onto the bandstand, pushing back his hair. Oddly enough, he didn't have his shoes on. Not the best thing for a drummer, I thought. But, hey, what did I know. Anyway, he just made it behind his drums as Tex counted off.

We opened the set with one of Miller/Beneke's biggest hits, practically a household name, "Chattanooga Choo Choo." The crowd loved it and cheered as we began. The dance floor swarmed once again with eager, sweaty flesh.

After the eight-bar intro, complete with train whistle effect, and the initial sax section first chorus, Tex began singing the tune's memorable lyric, just as he had on the original Miller recording, with his distinctive closed-throat, nasal style and wide vibrato. Compared to singers like Sinatra, he had all the romantic appeal of a lumberjack singing "Tenderly" while sawing down a Redwood.

I never understood in those days why Tex was personally such a hit with audiences. He had a rough, unpolished voice. But he was truly one of the vocal originals of the big band era. Now I can understand how he made fans feel at home and relaxed, like he was a regular guy. Because he was.

"Pardon me, Boy, is that the Chattanooga Choo Choo? Track 29. Well you can give me a shine."

The dancers sang right along with him. It was a fun tune with an infectious beat. During Eddie Zandy's trumpet solo I noticed that both the local lovelies, looking like toy dolls, were dancing with their too-tall Texans, all smiles, probably sweet-talking their men. But all the while they were looking past them, over to the band, making eyes at their two musician dandies, who, noticing they were being noticed, began playing with an extra bit of showmanship. There's nothing like the attention of admirers to make you feel appreciated and want to perform with extra spark.

"Hermie," I said, leaning over to him "Vinny better watch out, or he's going to get popped." Hermie merely shrugged. It was none of his business.

The next tune was "Skylark," a beautiful ballad by Hoagy Carmichael, composer of "Stardust." It had a challenging solo that really showed off the alto sax… and me. I loved playing it and played it well. Nobody cheered when I finished, but a quiet "That was nice," came from Hermie when I sat down again. Thanks, Hermie.

Six more tunes followed. By the time we got to the set-closer, "American Patrol," the crowd was practically levatating off the floor. In their whoop-it-up party mood, fueled by alcohol and by just plain pent-up energy, they demonstrated an aspect of group dynamics I hadn't observed before.

We had just finished Patrol when the fight broke out. And what a fight it was.

CRASH. SMASH. BAM. WHACK. Yelling. Fists connecting. Bodies colliding. Everyone seemed to be involved. It was a group melee. But I swear some people were laughing.

When the first bottle hit the chicken wire in front of us with a sudden wangggg, it scared the hell out of me. I was sitting, right in the middle of the front row. More bottles followed. Wangggg, wangggg, wangggg—empties, I would surmise, judging from the state of the crowd, though the thought didn't occur to me at the time, I was just trying to duck. We were caught in the middle of a good ole Texas Saturday-night brawl.

"This is it, huh Hermie," I said. "This is what Tex meant?"

"You got it, man."

Each bottle that hurtled toward us bounced harmlessly onto the slack chicken wire screen, before rolling down, and clanking onto the concrete.

"That's it, guys, Tex said calmly. "Pack it up."

I froze, open-mouthed. I thought for sure we might be killed. Maybe the crowd would charge the bandstand. I clutched my beautiful Selmer Alto close to me and ducked. But Tex was cool and matter-of-fact, as if it were a rehearsal. We had played only half the time for which we had been contracted, since the dance was supposed to go till midnight. But the old-timers on the band were already grabbing their horns and music and beating it out the back door onto the bus—which, I discovered, was warmed up, cooled down and ready to roll.

Most nights it took us about an hour to strike the set, putting away horns and equipment, hanging around and loading up the bus. And that was if we were in a hurry to get on the road to make it to the next town, check in, and get some sleep. Musicians don't move too fast after playing a gig. They like to mill around and unwind.

This time it couldn't have been more than fifteen minutes before we were out of there. All the while, the brawl continued inside with merry abandon. We changed out of our tuxes on the bus. No one seemed to be too upset, but I was shaking my head in disbelief. A crazy scene. *So this is the road,* I thought.

That's when Hermie told me this happens every year the band plays in Longview.

"You're kidding," I said. "Then why does Tex play here?"

"Because every year they offer him more money to come back. And they always pay in advance. It's the best paying date on the tour. And we never have to play more than half the gig before the fight starts."

About that time we heard some insistent pounding and yelling on the outside of our Greyhound. "Laura! Missy Mae! Laura!" The giants were stalking along the outside of the bus, actually looking *down* into the windows.

"Laura. Come outta there!" one of them, yelled. "I know you're in there!"

"You too, Missy Mae, " said the other..."Come out now, gol-damit, 'fore I turn this shit bus over." He probably could have.

It seems that the 'butterfly girls,' had accepted invitations from Dandie Duke and Vinny and managed to flit onto the bus during the big brawl and were now hiding. The two bruisers were prowling back and forth outside the bus like hound dogs stalking quail. Most likely they were sniffing for Duke and Vinny also—probably to rearrange their noses — pounding their fists against the side of the bus as they walked. I was getting anxious, but I decided to keep my mouth shut and see how the scene played out. As it turned out, this was one of my more prudent decisions.

Suddenly an angry face topped with a Stetson, was staring through one of the closed windows at Duke, who was slumped in his seat, bent over laughing, while the sweet, young lovely named Laura, was on the floor in front of him, apparently massaging his crotch, giggling.

Seeing Duke, the mad-faced Stetson guy yelled, "You little sonnovabitch. I'll break your ass!" He smacked his fist against the window. It didn't break. Suddenly Duke wasn't laughing. He slid down onto the floor between the seats.

"Oh, honey," the Texas bimbette said to Duke, "don't mind Hank. He's just jealous."

"No shit," said Vinny, sitting across the aisle with Missy Mae on his lap. "You girls better get off the bus," his words confirming, as I suspected, that he was the more practical of the two musicians. Clearly, he didn't want his mouth re-arranged.

The fist-pounding got more intense. The Giants were mad as hell and swaying-drunk—a couple of Jacks had climbed the Beanstalk, and were making off with the golden eggs.

Tex Beneke, the great white Texas oracle, who might have interceded, wasn't there, having already left in his '55 yellow Caddie convertible and well on his way by now to whatever town was next on the tour. He didn't travel on the bus with the band, neither did his wife. She drove a red Thunderbird. The two of them bantered back and forth on the road via their CB radios.

"Jesus, let's get out of here," said Zandy, who had been with the band for over five years. He wasn't known for risk-taking. The guys respected him. I guess he didn't want his embouchure adjusted by some crazy cowboys either.

Eddie Matthews spoke up. "You girls gotta get off now. I mean you have to leave the bus right now. We gotta go, and you can't come. Come on now, girls. Out! Now!"

With that the driver swung the door open. The girls gave the dandies long sloppy, liquor-soaked, lipstick-smeared smooches. Uck.

"Hurry up, for crissakes," Eddie said.

The big guys were making their way around the front of the bus toward the door.

"Come on girls," Eddie yelled. "Out. Now!"

Calling out. "Bye, fellas," the two femme fatales alighted, apparently unfazed, then faced their awaiting cowboys.

"Now Hank, honey," the one named Laura said. "We was just havin' some fun, some harmless fun. So doncha' go gettin' yourself all upset now."

Seymour slammed the door shut and gunned the motor a few times, just to let everyone know we were leaving. The two "trees" were shaking serious fists toward where they figured Duke and Vinny were sitting. The girls were clinging to their guys' arms, doing their 'we-got-to-soothe-our-stupid-but-necessary-men' tap dance. It appeared they knew the steps well.

It was time to move. As we drove off in a cloud of dust, Frank Huggins, the carefree lead trumpet player, yelled "Hi Ho Silver! Away!"

Duke and Vinny sat together and chuckled over their escape from the jaws of justice. Duke got out his little black book and started discussing possibilities for the next town. The man was dedicated.

Hermie opened a book to read. Zandy and some of the guys started a card game in the back. Frank was sipping a pint of gin through a straw while reading aloud to no one in particular from Downbeat magazine. Eddie Matthews was sitting up front schmoozing the singer, telling her how he could get her a recording deal after the tour was over.

I was a slim 130 pounds at the time, and 5'7". I climbed up into the shallow overhead luggage rack, flattened a small pillow, stretched out on my back, and settled in for the all-night drive to wherever. While studying the ceiling, inches away from my nose, I asked myself if this was turning out to be the glamorous career I imagined traveling on the road with a famous name band would be.

I listened to Duke and Vinny compare notes and to Frank reading away and laughing with sheer enjoyment at Downbeat's penchant for hyperbolic descriptions of idolized jazz musicians. I could overhear Eddie working his I'm-really-an-important-guy routine on the 'girl' singer. Random jokes from the poker game filtered up to me. And the bus lurched down the highway into the night.

I thought, how lucky I was to have made it. I was playing with a name band.

*

And that's all you thought?

(Well, there was a little more.)

Yes, I thought how lucky I was to have made it. But although I appreciated the opportunity immensely, something was missing. This was not the way to fame and fortune, and certainly not the way I wanted to spend my life, especially with a family. This road leads nowhere. Sooner or later you're right back where you started. I would have to think very carefully before touring again.

**

Nine

RHAPSODY IN BLUE

Repeatedly he banged the baton against the conductor's music stand until the stick shattered. "Goddammit, who's playing the clarinet solo?" he growled.

A hush swept over the orchestra, as if fanned by a silent wind. "I am," I said, ears burning at being singled out. Heart pounding. *Who does he think he is, Toscanini?*

The afternoon rehearsal of the Connecticut Symphony Summer Pops Concert was thus interrupted by its guest conductor, the famous Paul Whiteman.

The summer after the tour with the Tex Beneke Band I was asked to play the outdoor Pop series with the Connecticut Symphony. Although I was primarily an alto saxophonist, which was the reason they hired me, in classical circles I was called a doubler, that is, I 'doubled' on sax, clarinet, flute and piccolo, something that's par for the course for many pop/jazz woodwind players. But for most symphony musicians, who focus a lifetime on perfecting facility on a single instrument, the term carried with it the implication that a doubler, ipso facto, could not be outstanding on any single instrument. However, he might be considered 'acceptable' on those he played.

Even though the term's negative connotation was fading, there was still a *sub rosa* stigma attached to it, as in, "Oh, he plays well enough, I guess, but of course he's a doubler."

I was sensitive to this and frankly didn't like it. Although I never had the discipline to practice hours and hours perfecting the technique required to be a polished classical performer, I knew about swing and rhythm, sight-reading, phrasing, style, tone, how to blend with an ensemble, and improvisation. I knew I was an experienced and competent professional. So when I got the call, I was anxious to show the classical guys just how well a doubler could play. I took it as a challenge.

The afternoon of the concert, I drove to rehearsal at Fairfield University Field in high spirits—windows down, warm wind blowing in my face, singing along with the radio. I felt good after the stint with Beneke. A major career goal had been attained and that was encouraging.

The outdoor facility could seat 8,000 people, not including the blanket crowd. Folding chairs were set up on the mown grass in hundreds of converging rows facing toward the stage. The roofed music shed, trimmed in dark green wood, was framed by tall pine trees. Flower boxes full of chrysanthemums decorated the front of the stage floor. On the ground in front of the six-foot high stage, tall, potted ferns swayed in a gentle breeze. To the audience the symphony musicians must have appeared suspended, framed in a garden of greenery.

The opening half of the program featured Paul Whiteman, an American music icon, conducting the works of George Gershwin: "A Gershwin Medley" followed by "An American In Paris" and finally "Rhapsody In Blue." Johnny Mathis was the featured performer for the second half of the concert.

When I sat down behind my music stand and thumbed through Whiteman's music, I saw that the solo clarinet cadenza, which opens "Rhapsody In Blue" – starting with a trill on a low G and followed by a long, tricky glissando to a high D—was scored in this arrangement to be played on clarinet by the lead saxophonist (the doubler) and not by the orchestra's first chair classical clarinetist.

Now I was even more excited. It would be a welcome challenge. And what an honor it would be to play the clarinet solo conducted by Paul Whiteman, the man who had actually commissioned the original work. The Rhapsody had premiered in 1924 by Whiteman and had become an enduring classic, known worldwide; and the clarinet glissando opening was like the signature of the piece. And to think this was happening right in my hometown area with the symphony. How many pop musicians get to do something like that in their lifetime? I was psyched.

But the feeling didn't last long. Right at the start of the rehearsal, as Whiteman (with a theatrical overhead flourish) attempted to give the initial downbeat for the Gershwin medley—the first piece we were to rehearse—he slipped off his high stool, knocking his music stand from the podium. The score went sprawling, as he landed on his corpulent butt. Wow, what happened? Maybe he's sick?

He was a large, graying, bald man, baggy-eyed and pear-shaped, with the tired, sanguine look of a man trying to squeeze a few more years out of past glories. His pencil thin black moustache, the length of his upper lip, resembled the look of an old-fashioned movie actor. The stash was like a dark latitude marker across the middle of his high fore-headed map.

He shook it off without comment and recovered his composure. We began again. A couple of minutes into the medley he stopped the orchestra abruptly and began to rail at the drummer, getting redder and redder by the second.

"Dammit, drummer," he snarled, "What's the matter with you? Can't you read notes?"

I could feel the orchestra getting uneasy. We knew then it was going to be a long afternoon.

"Play it again," Whiteman groused. "And this time play it right,"

We started over, only to have him stop again almost immediately. "Jesus," he said shaking his head, "that's not it. What do you think you're doing, buddy? Take it again from the top. And play it like it's supposed to be played! Understand?"

Silence from the drummer.

After stopping us a third time, he turned on his stool and yelled over to the stage manager, "Get on the phone and get my drummer Johnny up here right away from New York."

This guy's going to blow a serious fuse, I thought. That kind of anger isn't good for you. We didn't rehearse any more of the Gershwin medley. The truth was, no one could follow his direction. He couldn't manage to count off in time, or give a recognizable downbeat, or conduct with authority or clarity, so tempo changes were a guess at best. It was as if he expected the orchestra to know the arrangements. Even though he wasn't showing us much respect, we were trying to be polite. After all, he was Paul Whiteman. We wanted to respect him. Even though at one time he was incorrectly known as the "King of Jazz", he had been a great innovator. Besides, he was old. *Why does he need his own drummer? Maybe he can't conduct?*

We managed to get through the next piece, "An American In Paris", without incident, though he continued to make sour faces when tempo changes apparently didn't seem quite perfect to him. The orchestra played it beautifully, but all around me the feeling was tense.

"Rhapsody In Blue" was next. I had never played the famous clarinet solo before, but I was vaguely familiar with it. It was short. Nothing to it. The only thing was, the clarinet starts the Rhapsody all alone. You're there completely exposed, with your bare tone hanging out, so to speak.

I wasn't quite sure what Whiteman wanted when, while he was looking off to the side of the stage, he sent out an off-handed wave in the general direction of the woodwind section. There was no cue, no downbeat. So nothing happened. No one played anything. He looked back, grimaced and yelled, "Alright, PLAY!" With that he waved his baton wildly at the woodwinds, apparently indicating that the solo clarinet cadenza should start NOW. So I began playing it, note for note, exactly as it was written on the manuscript.

That's when he threw his second tantrum, banging his baton repeatedly against his stand, long after the orchestra had stopped, until it broke into pieces, one of which landed in the hair of a lovely young cellist seated directly in front of him. He was really out-of-sorts. I almost felt sorry for him. I shouldn't have.

"Goddammit," he bellowed, glaring at the woodwind section, his hands on his considerable hips. "Who's playing the clarinet solo?"

I could feel eighty pairs of musician eyes swing toward me like converging mini-spotlights. They knew who was playing the clarinet solo.

"I am, " I said, trying to sound relaxed, like it didn't matter. I wasn't going to let him bully me, as he had done to the drummer. I was a little sensitive to that kind of treatment.

"You ever hear my recording (hic) of "Rhapsody in Blue?" he slurred loudly, trying to stare me down.

Now I understand. He's...

"No, I haven't," I said clearly. I was polite, but a far cry from being humble.

"Well for Crissakes, go out and buy it!"

"OKAY, " I said, matter-of-factly. The situation was clear to me, as I'm sure it was to the other musicians. He had a problem. Even so, I was embarrassed. I felt that my reputation as a good musician was in jeopardy, and I couldn't let that happen. At the same time, I had no idea of what he really wanted to hear.

Following a break, we rehearsed with Johnny Mathis. His ✓ arrangements were fine and he was a perfect gentlemen. He was most appreciative, and so were we. After rehearsal I immediately drove to Zera's Music Land in Fairfield, with my clarinet and the music, and asked if they had Paul Whiteman's recording of "Rhapsody In Blue ".

I took the 12" LP into one of the audition booths and listened several times to the cadenza. Ah, I see. So that's it. It wasn't being played as scored in my music. The glissando was written out note-for-note, with no indication of it being connected into one long upward slide. It was a copyist error. I took out my clarinet and played along with the record several more times until I had it. I'd show that has-been turkey tonight.

Fifteen minutes before concert time I was seated on stage in my white dinner jacket, silently fingering the clarinet solo. Other musicians were warming up. A couple of them said to me, "Everything okay, Gene?"

"Yeah, sure. No problem, " I said. *See? I knew some of them would be concerned over whether I could play it right. Doubler, they probably thought.*

The July night clearly showed the starry roof of heaven. It was beautiful. Though the field had been sprayed that afternoon and again an hour before the concert, some of God's little bitties were hovering – it was still buggy. Soon the lights dimmed. It was time.

When Whiteman walked on stage, he seemed to have recovered from the afternoon's disaster. I could only hope. Surprisingly, the program went well. Before his final number, "Rhapsody in Blue," he went to the microphone—resplendent in his size 48-long, white dinner jacket, red bow tie, and red cummerbund—and told the story of how he had asked

"George" to compose something different for his orchestra "a composition that would be both classical and jazz."

"The result, ladies and gentlemen," he went on to say with grand pomp, "Rhapsody In Blue, a composition that I had the privilege of premiering at Aeolian Hall in New York City over thirty years ago. Of course the rest is history." He paused. The audience applauded warmly. You would have thought he had composed the Rhapsody himself.

When he turned around and faced the orchestra, my clarinet was already at my lips, waiting for his downbeat, or gesture, or whatever sign might come my way. I could feel the tension in the orchestra building. The audience hushed. He raised his baton.

At that precise moment there was a terrifying scream from a woman somewhere out in the crowd. It cut the night like lightning slices darkness. She kept screaming, running wildly though the audience toward the stage, apparently hysterical. The audience stilled. Her screams smothered even the silence. Ushers froze where they stood. Special police ran to her aid and carried her, still screaming, to an ambulance that was kept parked behind the stage.

It was terrible. What had happened? The crowd was now buzzing. I was supposed to be ready to play the cadenza. I tried to re-focus my concentration.

Whiteman had stood to the side of the stage, partly facing us, watching the interrupting drama unfold. When it was over, smiling graciously to us and then to the audience, he shrugged with understanding, as if to say "Oh well, what can you do?" then returned to center stage. The crowd applauded. They were with him.

When he turned to the orchestra, I made it a point to look right at him, so he'd know I was ready to go. I wasn't going to screw up this moment, screams or no screams. He smiled broadly at me. Huh? He indicated that I should stand up for the solo. When the audience had quieted completely, he gave me a little nod, a raised eyebrow, an expression that said, "Ready?" I affirmed with a serious nod. He tapped briskly on his music stand two short tics's with a new baton, raised his arms, then gave me a precise stroke to begin.

I hesitated for a millisecond.

In that instant I could sense panic grip the musician next to me. Sometimes my mind does wander. He nudged my arm with his elbow just as I was starting to play. I guess he was afraid I would be late playing the cue. I blew into my horn at the same time I was jostled. A terrible squawking squeak came out. Whiteman became enraged. He must have thought I was making fun of him. The audience amused themselves with snickers. He came over to my stand and ordered me off the stage. I got up and left, totally embarrassed. It was six months before I'd play again. Eventually I moved to a different city.

*

*Oh my, you really do have a flair for the dramatic.
A squawking squeek? Get real.*

(Heh, heh, just kidding, you know.)

Do me a favor. Tell it like it was.

I hesitated for a millisecond, put the screams out of my head, then proceeded to deliver the cadenza with conviction, exactly the way Whiteman wanted it. From the first note I could feel the tone I was producing resonating out from the stage with power, grace and sureness. I felt one with the music, realizing that rare moment of perfect synergy. You live for such moments. You dream about them. A sensation like no other exultation fills your being. I was helping to create a first rate happening in music. When I finished, Whiteman smiled a raised-eyebrow "Thank you," nodded, and conducted the rest of the piece comfortably. His regular drummer was playing in the orchestra, and that relaxed him.

With a gracious bow he took the generous applause of the audience, then swept his arm back to the fine piano soloist, who took well-deserved accolades and then gestured over to me. He then recognized the whole orchestra with a gallant sweep. I was proud of myself. I had done a professional job.

Even though he had put us through hell that afternoon, by evening he had gathered himself together and had performed with the charisma the audience expected of a man of his reputation.

It was an enlightening experience, and I was glad I had done well. Even so, I still thought he was an ass.

The next day we found out that the screaming young woman, still in hospital, had reason to be upset. A buzzing Japanese beetle had crawled deep into her ear canal.

Poor woman; she never got to hear my little solo.

**

Ten

THE MUSICIANS CLUB

"You don't sound so bad for a white guy," Tiny said, after I finished playing a few 'ad-lib' choruses on "Comin' Home Baby." I appreciated the compliment. Tiny was a bass player and organized the jam sessions at the Musicians Club. Short, very wide – a "Mister Five by Five" type—dark skinned, red-haired, he had a calm way about him that was easy to like. I liked him even more after his compliment.

The Musicians Club was a dive, but it was a great place to jam once in a while, especially for me at this time in my life. I was pleased with my development as a lead alto saxophonist and multi-reed professional, and had gained a respected reputation in the business. However, I wanted to improve my improvisational skills.

When you're learning new things you sometimes have to let go of what you feel secure with in order to grow, especially when you're trying to develop new musical techniques—the early results usually don't sound too wonderful, so there's not much to encourage you. Improvisation is quite a different skill from reading music. You can't read it. You have to create it. An instant synergy between ear and playing what you hear has to occur. Developing this facility can be humbling. It takes time; there is no short-cut. However, the process of improving is often its own reward and the leap into new ideas usually brought me lasting pleasure and energy. I sensed this was the time and place for me to take the leap.

I was off the road for good, I thought. No more Ted Lewis stuff. No more corny music. Or Texas dance hall brawls. No more trying to sleep every other night in luggage racks on one-nighter buses. No more schlepping luggage and horns into cheap hotels, checking out half asleep, forgetting socks, underwear, razors, alarm clocks, toothbrushes, wallets—once even a watch. And no more separations from my family.

My kids hardly knew me anymore. I thought when I returned from the road I could take up being a father and husband right where I left off. But it wasn't so easy. My children were confused. They constantly deferred to their mother. I became impatient and would yell at them out of frustration. I never used to do that. "You're mean, Daddy," one of my daughters once said, when I told her "No more television, it's time to go to bed," not knowing it was a special program for her.

"Be patient, Gene," my wife said, "They have to get used to your being home again. It'll take a little time."

I understood. But it hurt. My ego was in crisis. I was no longer the *Grande Fromage*. I didn't like the minor role that I had been newly assigned. *I'm home now. And I'm staying. I'm their father. Don't they understand?* I knew I would make progress toward being a better father if I slowed down and let things happen naturally. So I did. However, the matter of my career would never leave my head.

During the day I was working full time for WICC Radio as an account executive, a euphemism for commercial time salesman. Not that I thought of myself as a salesman. Nor did I think of radio as a career. I was a musician, always looking for ways to make music my life's work. It was dishonest, I admit. I couldn't commit to the station job the way the owners had a right to expect.

When I signed up a new account on my first day in the field, they told me I could "move up quickly in this industry." However, the prospects of a career in radio, while more interesting than retailing, didn't seem to promise the same personal fulfillment as music. So, along with learning how to be successful on the job, I knew I needed to continue developing my arsenal of musical skills.

On weekends I played club dates and weddings – sometimes I'd have three or four small bands working under my name on a Saturday night. I'd make the rounds, play a set here, shake hands there, and collect the checks. In the meantime I kept cultivating New York City contacts, once in a while getting a call to play on a record date or a commercial with people like Doc Serverinsen, Clark Terry, Herbie Hancock, Gato Barbieri, Angelo DiPippo, Ron Carter and Ed Shaunessey. Studies with Joe Allard in New York continued, as well as practicing my horns an hour each day. I wrote and recorded a TV score for a ten-minute cartoon pilot called Billy Bounce. It was good. I liked it. The producers did too. It didn't get sold. We were getting by…barely.

During this decade, I also substituted occasionally on 'replacement nights' with traveling name bands like Billy May, Duke Ellington, Charlie Speak, Buddy Morrow, and Dick Stabile. I heard about Thursday night jam sessions at the Bridgeport Colored Musicians Union located on South Main Street, and went there to learn, by listening to other musicians and sitting-in with them. In jam sessions you can tell right away where your weaknesses are.

When Tiny asked me to play there regularly with the house band, I told him I'd love to.

"Pays twelve to fifteen, depending on how many door admissions that night," he said. "Admission is a dollar." Obviously money was not the motivation for me playing there—although every little bit helped. As Duke Ellington wrote, "It Don't Mean a Thing If It Ain't Got That Swing." And that's what this place was all about. No waltzes or polkas or country club music. Just straight up blues and jazz.

In the 1950's the American Federation of Musicians was a segregated union. In Bridgeport, the white Local #63, had a spacious hall downtown, where there were monthly meetings, lots of card games… and no jam sessions. It collected a ten percent 'traveling tax' from all musicians and bands that came into the city's jurisdiction to play – even for one night—as did most locals at that time.

If you were a professional, you had to belong to the union or you couldn't work. It was run by a few older cronies who mostly played poker and smoked cigars in the meeting hall. Sure, they had instruments, but didn't play them much any more, except maybe for a Labor Day band concert in the park. I was a young rebel and didn't respect them. As far as I was concerned the union was not about music.

The 'Colored Local' on the other hand, as it was called by everyone, even its own members, had this funky, quasi-nightclub meeting hall called the Musicians Club.

The club was a third floor walk-up over a wholesale plumbing supply store in the industrial end of town. A wide, double flight of wooden stairs with a landing halfway up was the only way to get there. It was a long flight. I counted once, thirty-eight steps. But the hike was worth it.

The club had swinging music three nights a week and after-hours jam sessions on a fourth night. It featured a shot-and-a-beer bar for the drinkers, and the most relaxed collection of partiers I'd ever seen. But mostly the scene was about the music.

Customers, no matter what ethnic background, usually dressed up when they came here. Even the musicians in the band wore jackets and ties. The place itself was rather stark, with linoleum floors and fluorescent light fixtures covered with red crepe paper. The small wooden dance floor had been painted red ...obviously often; a fresh coat was added as the floor became scuffed and faded. If paint had ever been applied to the walls, it had long since retreated into the pores of the wallboard. Not a mirror or a picture was hung to interrupt the drabness.

None of that mattered to the folks who came there, because it was theirs. It was their place to hang out, a place where they could make as much noise as they wanted, play the music they wanted, and raise general hell when they so chose. This unpretentious place was a musical Mecca for musicians interested in developing improvisation abilities.

The club had a capacity of about 150 people. It was dark, and sexy in a way—though pretty loud at times. A dozen or so wooden tables and chairs surrounded the dance floor. There was little racial animosity shown toward its few white patrons, and especially not to musicians. Nobody much bothered you. Once in a rare while, police came to break up a fight, or because occasionally somebody got quietly knifed "a little"—usually in a dispute over whose mistress was with whom. "He be dancing so close she be on the other side of him, that's why I cut him."

Every night a different group played, usually four or five guys, most all of whom belonged to the Colored Union. A few of us 'grays' went up there on Thursdays to sit in and jam. It was usually joyous, rockin', swinging, straight-ahead music. The place was cool, especially if you could really play.

However, if you were a fake and tried to pass yourself off as a player, even if you managed to blow a few flashy 'licks' you 'copped' off a Charlie Parker or Cannonball Adderley record, they'd know it soon enough. They'd figure you were trying to be "in" with the "folks." And it didn't work.

For instance, you could wear the coolest suit and hippest tie and have the latest 'shades' on, and sling phrases around like, "Yeah Man, I'm hip," or "Like, crazy, man." But if what came out of your horn when you played didn't live up to your affectations, then watch out. These folks knew good notes from bad notes. It was their thing. They listened. Music mattered. Even if couples were dancing wrapped around each like ficus plants, they'd still be listening to the band.

One night I was playing at Guest Night, standing along side Ray Duseki, a white musician sitting in on tenor sax for a set. We were on the slightly elevated bandstand at one end of the room, opposite the bar. It was a narrow platform, about ten feet long and six feet deep. Behind it were large floor-to-ceiling windows, covered with heavy brown paper, facing the street below. A couple of small red spotlights, screwed into the ceiling in front of the mini stage, were aimed at the bandstand.

I finished playing a few choruses on "Walkin' the Blues" — played it simple and uncomplicated, trying to make it swing. I would have played more impressively if I could have. But hell, that was why I was there. When I finished, there were a few modest "All right"s, "Uh huh"s, and "I hear you" from dancers nearby. I felt good about that. I knew I was getting there.

I was making progress. Or maybe they were just being kind. Then it was Ray's turn. He proceeded to blow at least fifteen choruses on his tenor, one after the other, each of which seemed to be filled with a thousand notes. He was dressed in a gray sharkskin, double-breasted suit with a blue shirt and black knit tie and pointed black shoes, looking like he was a serious cat. He had all the right moves—the swaying, the eyes shut, the elbows flapping, the horn raised up toward the ceiling for a few bars, and the climactic knee squats, denoting special emotional involvement at certain highlights of his solo—all of which added to his image as a heavy player. Man, he looked like a heavy dude. But what he was playing didn't swing. Just notes were coming out. And everyone knew it. Except maybe Ray. He didn't stop soloing.

The dancers stopped dancing and started grumbling. It was the first time I ever heard "*sh-it*" pronounced as a two-syllable word. I liked it. Usually if a guy didn't cut it when he sat in, no one said anything. They'd just glare at him until he got the message.

However, this time wide-man-Tiny decided it was just too much. While the drummer and pianist kept playing, he put down his bass and bulged up to Ray. "Whoa, man," he said, "You know what your problem is? You so hip, you hoppin' over what's happenin'. Take a break. Sit down and listen. Or go home and practice."

It wasn't a sensitive thing to do. I felt bad for Ray. But I sensed that Tiny's integrity was on the line with the folks who were watching. He probably figured that if he didn't do something now, they'd let him know about it later.

Nobody else said anything. Ray put his horn in his case and walked to the door, sensing, I'm sure, the chill he was getting from the crowd. He couldn't seem to get out of there fast enough.

It wasn't that his playing was unimpressive—some people don't play well. But because he came on with all the accoutrements and attitude of an important dude, then didn't play, the crowd marked him as a 'jive-ass, honky no-talent'. It was *vox populi*. Thumbs down. An instantaneous judgment. Tiny would probably dis-invite him if he ever showed up again.

After Ray left, Tiny turned to me, as if to apologize, and said, "The man thinks flashy playing is music."

I nodded in agreement.

In this place music was a meritocracy. Like sports, the best players got the most respect. Bad ones didn't get any. I figured I was just a utility player in this league.

GENE HULL

And then there was Hank Conroy—everyone knew him as Zeke—the piano player playing the gig most nights. Zeke was white, tall, lanky, brown-haired, wore glasses and played great. He'd been around and had street savvy.

One night I was in the middle of playing "Misty" on the alto, a nice slow ballad, trying to make it sound warm and sexy and honest. Folks on the floor were dancing belly to belly. I had shut my eyes. I was into it. "Play 'Sweet Georgia Brown,'" I heard a gruff voice say.

I opened my eyes. Several people were close to the bandstand. I couldn't tell who spoke. We kept playing and I looked over at Zeke. He shrugged, like he couldn't care less who was requesting what. I resumed playing "Misty" and closed my eyes again doing my reverie thing. I heard the voice again, this time louder.

"Play 'Sweet Georgia Brown.'" I looked up and there was this thin, woozy, red-eyed guy with stinking breath swaying right in front of my face. He had no eyelashes, and his eyes seemed to be focused somewhere between here and there. He was drunk or drugged, or both.

But damn it, I thought, drunk or not this guy was way out of line. I was there to play real music and not to contend with jerks. Besides, since I had a few friends around the club who liked me, I decided to handle the situation with acceptable righteous indignation.

"Hey, Man, be cool," I said. "We'll play your tune right after this one." That sounded reasonable to me. Maybe I did have a bit of attitude showing. But hey, what's right is right. The guy should have been straightened out. And I figured it was up to me to do it.

I stopped playing, backed away and shot him some 'rays.' Right away Zeke picked up the melody I had abandoned. He played it beautifully on the beat-up upright piano, the thumb and little finger of his right hand spreading out to play the melody in octaves, as if Errol Garner were there in person. I loved listening to Zeke.

The next thing I knew, a five-inch switchblade knife clicked out from the guy's hand and assumed a strategic position just below Zeke's left ear. "Play 'Sweet Georgia Brown,'" the geek said to the back of Zeke's head. The blade caught the light just so, and for a moment flashed like a mirror. I didn't know what to do. Dumbfounded, I didn't move.

Zeke froze. The geek plunged the knife into Zeke's shoulder. Blood spilled like a slow garden hose. Zeke fell to the floor. The knifer turned to me, waved the bloody blade. I jumped back, grabbed a folding chair from the bandstand and threw it at him. He lost his balance for a moment. One of the dancers jumped on his back. Dragged him to the floor. More piled on, punching him, kicking him mercilessly. A nurse in the crowd first-aided Zeke, who by then was sitting up, dazed, wondering what had happened. He looked at the floor, shook his head slowly, and managed to say weakly, "I never did like that tune." Police came, arrested and cuffed the assailant and took him away. Zeke was brought to the hospital in a police car. The musicians and I packed up our instruments and left. Zeke recovered.

*

Gene, would you mind replaying that knife scene? This time with film in the camera?

(Okaaaay, so it didn't happen quite like that.)

The blade caught the light just so, and for an instant flashed like a mirror. I didn't know what to do. Dumbfounded, I froze.

Without missing a beat or even turning around to see who said it, Zeke immediately aborted "Misty" and ripped into an up-tempo solo stride—piano version of "Sweet Georgia Brown," as loud as he could play it—sounding like a mechanical piano in a shooting gallery. The man nodded, walked away, and mingled in with the crowd. The rest of us joined in and jammed out on the newly selected tune.

I was shaken up. I could have been slashed, or worse—and I knew it. I forgot where I was. I was a guest here. I should have been more careful. I could just see the newspapers, "Local Musician, Father of Four, Stabbed in Musicians Club Over 'Sweet Georgia Brown.'"

Zeke's quick thinking averted what could have been a messy situation. We all forced a laugh when we finished the song and took a break. Zeke said, "Where'd he go?"

"You shoulda' listened to the man," Tiny said to me casually.

"Sh-it!" I said. " If that guy ever comes in here again and asks for a tune, I'll give him a 'Yes, Sir' so fast he'll think he's God *and* Charlie Parker."

They laughed. I laughed, too. But I was serious. I never thought music could be so important that I might get stabbed over it. I guess there's more than one way to get your favorite tune played.

I learned a lot about concepts of swing and time and honest notes at the Musicians Club, which is what I set out to do. I also learned that jazz is a lot like life—if you don't have anything to say, shut up.

Since those days, whenever my mouth is about to get me into trouble, I try humming a few bars of "Sweet Georgia Brown." Sometimes it helps.

**

Eleven

WHITE FLASH

"You mean Kathěrine Hepburn, *the* Kathěrine Hepburn?" I said.

That's right," said lean Mike Donato, the theater's musician contractor. "Now would you play this cadenza?" He wasn't asking.

A symphony clarinetist might have known the passage, but I had never seen it. So I just plowed straight ahead and played the notes, sight-reading fairly correctly, but not yet fully understanding its flow and how it should be phrased. I knew I could do much better with a second crack at it. "Let me try that again," I said apologetically, yet with enough enthusiasm to show my confidence.

"No, that won't be necessary." He quickly removed the music from the stand. "Now play some of this Mozart Concerto. Start at the *con brio* section, right here." He pointed to a place on the music he had just opened up. "Ready?" Again, it wasn't a question. Without hesitating, he began conducting the tempo using a pencil as a baton.

It seemed fast, even for a *con brio* marking. Too fast. Too many notes. Damn. I'm making too many mistakes. What is this, a race?

Mike stopped me before I got through half a page and gave me a narrow look, pursing his lips, rolling his eyes, arching his overgrown brows, and putting on a 'how plebian' expression—as if I had tried to tell him a tired joke. I let it pass. This was not the time to take issue, though his attitude did gall me. He was a symphony musician, and he knew I wasn't. To him I was, therefore, not up to his standards. For some reason he was out to prove the point. He didn't know what he didn't know.

The theater's 1958 season required an alto saxophonist who could double A-flat and B-flat clarinets and flute for its pit orchestra. Since I was the most accomplished multi-reed player in the area, and was asked to audition, I figured the audition was more or less a mere formality.

However, after I played the Mozart, Donato put on a labored, 'I-told-you-so' smirk and inclined his condescension to the other fellow on the 'audition committee,' violist Louie Cappucci.

Affable Louie, seemingly content in his caloricly-challenged physique, shrugged at Donato, as if to say, 'So, he didn't play it perfectly, but it really wasn't that bad.'

"Gene, Louie said, "Try the cadenza again? And this time relax. Take your time with it."

I played it with more understanding of its proper phrasing, not just producing correct notes. It flowed. I liked it.

"Good," he said, "now take the beginning of the Mozart again, not quite so fast."

It was much better than the first time.

"Okay. Now, play a tune you know on the sax, anything you like, something that shows your tone and phasing."

"Sure," delivering a confident, if slightly slurpy, version of Duke's "I Got It Bad And That Ain't Good", ala Johnny Hodges, the foremost exponent of the gushy romantic style. *Ah, this is more my element. I'm sounding real good now.*

Louie was smiling. Three quarters of the way through, he stopped me and said, "That's fine, Gene."

The two of them got up and walked to the far side of the room, conferring.

"So Katherine Hepburn's going to be in the cast, huh?" I called over to them, trying to divert their attention from dwelling on my mistakes. They didn't respond.

When they came back Donato offered dismissively, "Actually, she's the star. "

"My God, that's incredible. I mean... she's a great actress. And she's coming here to do the plays this season? Wow. How great." *Am I talking too much? I need this job. I don't want to blow it. I can cut it, if they give me a chance.*

"She's already here. The cast has been rehearsing for weeks," said Donato.

"But how come you're auditioning musicians? Is the play a musical? I never heard of Shakespeare done as a musical."

"No, this is legit Shakespeare," said Louie. "The music is incidental stuff, segues between scenes, at the end of acts, transition music, and a few original songs. Virgil Thompson wrote the score. He'll be here in person to rehearse the orchestra."

"Virgil Thompson?" I hadn't a clue.

"The producers commissioned him to compose it. They want the productions to be extra special this season," Fred said.

"I guess. Well, like, cool, man." What a nice guy, I thought.

Donato grimaced. "Hmm. Look, Gene"—indicating he was in charge again, thank you— "we think you can probably handle the music. So you've got the job. It pays scale. Don't forget you need to double both clarinets—B flat and A—and alto sax, of course.

"There are also a few flute and piccolo parts, but Claude Monteux is the principal flutist." He pronounced the name *Cloed*, as the French say it, instead of *Clawed*, like they might say it in Bridgeport. For a moment I didn't get it.

"Who," I said?

"Cloed Monteux... from the Concertgebouw?"

"Oh, the Concertgebouw?"

"The symphony orchestra from Amsterdam?" Louie offered.

"Oh, right." Again I was clueless. In those days I was into conductors like Stan Kenton, Count Basie, Woody Herman, Dizzy, Duke and Quincy Jones, and maybe Leonard Bernstein and Toscanini.

"Rehearsals start Wednesday next week," Donato said. "Eleven A.M. sharp." It was more like a challenge than an announcement.

"Right on, man. I'll be here. Thanks, guys."

And so I was hired to play in the orchestral ensemble for the summer/fall season at the American Shakespeare Festival Theater in Stratford, Connecticut, little realizing what would happen to me there. But first let me give you a picture of the place.

By every standard the theater was elegant. Designed as a modern interpretation of a classic olde theatre, it had a majestic façade of gray teak decorated with flying pennants, Coat of Arms plaques and several red-door entrances.

Nestled on twelve wooded acres amid tall elms on the banks of the Housatonic River in Stratford, about sixty-five miles from New York City, it was a handsome, full-stage, multi-purpose theatrical house, dedicated to performing works of Shakespeare.

Soon it captured the fancy of the American theatrical community from Broadway to Hollywood. Everyone wanted to be associated with it. A formidable cadre of famous actors and directors was assembled to develop and produce high-standard theater.

This year's acting company of over twenty principals included such names as Katherine Hepburn, Alfred Drake—star of "Kismet" on Broadway—and Maurice Carnovski, whose sensitive portrayal of Shylock left audiences breathless, plus two renowned directors: John Houseman—fresh from ~~directing~~ *Lust For Life* in Hollywood with Kirk Douglas and who later would direct and star in television's long running, successful series *The Paper Chase*—and Broadway's Jack Landau.

[margin notes: WRONG SPELLINGS; PRODUCING (VINCENTE MINNELLI DIRECTED IT)]

Without a doubt, however, Katherine Hepburn was the star. Her formidable charisma and artistry were the catalysts that ultimately established the theater's artistic standard—not to mention her considerable draw at the box office.

The stage was different from others I had seen up to then. It was raked in the tradition of an Elizabethan theatre, slanted downward toward the audience. The orchestra was situated under the stage, unseen by the audience, in a dark place I called the dungeon. From this location the music could be heard clearly throughout the house, and musicians could hear the stage action. It was possible to walk out from the dungeon into the pit, and watch the performers, unseen by the audience and un-noticed (I thought) by the actors on stage.

The dungeon itself was unlit, except for music stand lights and a single blue light that allowed us to find our places in the darkness. A small, red cue-light would go on at precisely ten seconds before the next music cue so we could prepare.

In a few weeks I settled into a routine. The music was easy and fun to play. But the long waits between cues began to be boring. To pass the time musicians would tinker with their instruments, replace a reed or a string, oil a key or read by the light of the music stands. Sometimes during these lulls, I would go over the fingering of a challenging clarinet passage. But most of the time I'd just sit there listening to the audience responding to whatever the actors stomping across the stage above were doing.

Eventually, I could identify the actors by the sound of their footsteps. In *Much Ado About Nothing* Larry Gates, who played Dogberry the Constable, had a heavy, slow, 'kalomp-kalomp-heelskuff' walk. I could tell Alfred Drake as Benedick right away as he moved across the stage with his confident, heel-toe strut that never seemed in a hurry. As for Miss Hepburn, who portrayed the feisty Beatrice, her shoes clicked as she walked, with the studied confidence of a woman who was clever, witty and self-assured. At the same time her steps seemed to have a girlish, buoyant quality, as if she were politely deferring to Benedick, yet demonstrating her independence from him. How did she do that? Listening, without seeing the actor's movements, gave me an appreciation of an aspect of acting technique I would never have noticed.

After several performances, I had my fill of recognizing the sound of actors' feet. I used the mini breaks to go out into the pit and watch snippets of the show, hidden from the audience by the wall that separates the pit from the house. What a rare opportunity to observe Miss Hepburn on stage, so close I could almost touch her. She was enchanting.

Every gesture, every accent, every movement seemed to shape her performance with precise nuance. It was masterful acting craftsmanship.

After a few nights of this, I found that by timing it just right and watching for the red cue light, I could remain watching the action until the last possible moment, then run back underneath the stage to the music stand, take up my instrument, just in time to play the next cue.

Donato didn't like my routine at all. "Hey Hotshot, You better not miss a cue. You're not here to watch the plays."

He was right, of course. *But, oh Donato, you're so dull. You're only thirty-nine, and already you're an old man. While you're reading the newspapers in the breaks, I'm getting a once-in-a-lifetime theater education. Get a life.*

Three plays were selected for production that season: *Othello*, *The Merchant of Venice*, in which Miss Hepburn's Portia was extraordinary, and *Much Ado About Nothing*, easily the audience's favorite. *Othello* and *Merchant* were staged in traditional, period Shakespearian costumes. In John Houseman's *Much Ado*, set in the American Southwest during the mid 1800's, the actors wore peasant tunics, sombreros, elegant Caballero outfits, boots, shawls, sandals, colorful flowing Mexican skirts and pastel lace dresses.

What made his direction particularly interesting for the musicians was that we had to be on stage in crowd scenes, once to play for the courtyard entrance of Don Pedro's army, and again in the beginning of the Finale to play for the cast waltz scene.

We were costumed in baggy white muslin 'peasant' pants, white muslin tunics with long, full sleeves, white neckerchiefs, sandals, and white rope ties for belts. Some of us wore sombreros.

Each day, before the day's performances, we arrived an hour early to apply moustaches, sideburns or beards with makeup gum, and get into full costume. The extras (including musicians) had 'lines' in one of the scenes—well, more accurately, cheering and yelling "yea, yeah, yea, hur-ray" over and over, creating the effect of a boisterous, happy crowd. For serious musicians, who usually seek refuge behind their instruments when required to be on-stage, this was heady stuff. They shied away from even the most basic acting attempts. They were uncomfortable with being on stage. Some of them froze when it was time to get into character, even as anonymous members of a Mexican crowd. Of course the audience was always focused on Katherine Hepburn or Alfred Drake, but the self-conscious musicians felt that everyone was looking at them. Naturally.

It was understandable, considering musicians spend years practicing their instruments umpteen hours a day, taking lessons, classes, studying, rehearsing, listening, schooling, and performing. They tend to take themselves seriously as artists. This was true with jazz players I had encountered along the way. Even serious college musicians hated to be in the school's marching band. But I found that professional classical musicians were even more fragile.

I understood the rationale. Their logic might have proposed, 'Would a brain surgeon be required to sing "The Very Thought Of You" to nurses while he was performing a frontal lobotomy? Would a university bio-physicist be expected to break out in a tap dance for his students in the lecture hall? So why should an accomplished musician be asked to act?'

Personally, I loved the performing aspect. In fact, I really got into it. As rehearsals proceeded, John Houseman could see my natural born ham-ism coming out and made me the front guy in the crowd. Maybe because I was the shortest? Naw.

Katherine Hepburn had propelled the company's performances to a high artistic level with much acclaim. You would think someone with such influence would be affected and difficult to deal with. But this was not the case. Between acts, and for an hour or so before curtain, and sometimes thereafter, there would be a large, friendly, backstage poker game, for quarters. Often she would sit in, smoke a cigarillo, and play a few hands with the stagehands and actors. She was fun to watch. No airs or attitude. Since I was not really part of the acting community, I would stand off a bit and observe, marveling at her one-of-the-guys rapport.

Just before the end of Scene iii, Act I, she had a brilliant soliloquy, which she delivered downstage center. I would leave the dungeon and go out into the pit to watch her. It was a pivotal point in the plot, when, overhearing others say that Benedick loved her deeply, Beatrice believes she has grossly misjudged him and decides to devote herself to him completely.

Her delivery of the speech stopped the show with applause every night. But try as I might to stay until the very end, I could not. The transition music to the next scene had to be played right after her soliloquy. I would watch till the last possible second before I'd dart back to play the cue.

There was a problem with my nightly trips into the pit. And it wasn't with Donato.

Sailors allude to a phenomenon called the green flash. In subtropical climates, a green light sometimes appears mysteriously on the horizon just as the sun sets. It's rare, but many people have seen it. However, as far I know, only one person has ever seen the *white flash*—Katherine Hepburn. Let me explain.

One night during her monologue I decided I would stay pit-watching her to the last split second before I had to get back to my music stand. This time I did manage to catch one more phrase or so before I had to make a run for it.

After the play, when the lights went up and the house was emptying, I put my horns in their cases and strolled into the backstage lounge to watch the fun. The stagehands and some of the actors were already ensconced in a lively hand of poker. Several of the cast were milling about, doing whatever actors do backstage after a performance, chatting, flirting, laughing, changing.

Suddenly Miss Hepburn came storming into the area in full costume, her eyes blazing, and demanded, "Who *the hell* is that in the pit when I'm doing the soliloquy?"

The room hushed. The poker game froze. Jokes suspended in mid punch lines. The musicians knew I was the one. No one breathed. Miss Hepburn searched faces around the room.

"Well?"

At length a barely audible voice emerged from a far corner. "It's me. I'm the one." It was my voice. But I didn't recognize it.

She stomped over to where I was standing in my white tunic, white pants, white rope belt and white neckerchief. "Well, just what *the hell* are you doing there?"

Even when she was mad—and she was—I loved the clipped way she separated her words and the nasal sound of her voice.

Everyone was looking at me. I saw Donato sneer at me, with an 'I-told-you-so, dumb ass', smirk. I deserved it. I wasn't feeling too smart then.

"I'm watching you do the soliloquy," I croaked.

"Yes, I gather that. What's your name?"

"Gene."

"Well damn it, Gene, if you're watching me why are you running back under the stage just when I'm getting close to the end of the piece? Don't you realize that breaks my concentration? Every night, just as I'm building to the climax, I see this *white flash* in my peripheral vision, practically under my nose, dashing back under the stage.

Oh my God, a white flash. Shit, I've been caught. And by Miss Hepburn, the star herself. She's talking at me and she's mad. I'll be fired. What'll I do? Please let me disappear right now.

"Do you have any idea of how terribly distracting that is?" Why on earth are you doing that?"

"I, I'm so sorry. I'm, I'm fascinated by your speech. I was just trying to see you do the end of it before I have to play the next music cue."

"Hmm I see."

Then a strange thing happened. I could no longer hear her. She was talking to me. I saw her lips moving. But I was fading away to another place. It must have been the stress. I do know that she took my hand, and we were walking.

Suddenly we were all alone in her dressing room and she was standing in costume right in front of me. "Now listen, she said." She then declaimed, in character, the ending lines of the noted soliloquy:

> *"And Benedick, love on; I will requite thee,*
> *Taming my wild heart to thy loving hand.*
> *If thou dost love, my kindness shall incite thee*
>
> *To bind our loves up in a holy band.*
> *For others say thou dost deserve, and I*
> *Believe it better than reportingly."*

"Will that do, Gene," She smiled easily right into my eyes.

"Oh my God, yes. Thank you, Miss Hepburn. Thank you. That's so kind of you. I'm such a fan of yours."

"Yes. I can see that."

I'm sure the poker game suspended while the players and everyone else stood amazed, listening through the door, as one of the greatest actresses of our time delivered the impassioned soliloquy of Act I for a private audience composed of one young, cocky musician no one had ever heard of.

What a special moment.

What a special lady.

*

There's more, isn't there?

(Ah… yes, a little.)

Well?

Curiously, her voice faded back in. I could hear her speaking naturally again. I looked around, I was standing in the cast lounge. There was Miss Hepburn standing next to me, still holding my hand and talking to me gently now.

"...and so you won't ever do that again, will you, Gene?"

"No, Miss Hepburn, I certainly won't. You can be sure of that," even more confused. Had I moved? Had she acted out the soliloquy for me in her dressing room? No one could tell me.

That night was the last time The White Flash went out into the pit to watch Katharine Hepburn. I continued to listen from the dungeon. But whenever she delivered the soliloquy, I could just see her, spinning a web, spellbinding the audience, consuming them, carrying them to another time and place, a moment of perfect theatre.

Well, did she or didn't she?

(Hmm.)

**

Twelve

THE JAZZ GIANTS

The Jazz Giants began as a fun project, a rehearsal band of professional musicians who wanted to play interesting big band arrangements. I had gathered together ex-professional players from the Connecticut area who shared this desire. We formed a creative ensemble called The Modern Music Workshop. The name helped to create an image of musicians-on-a-mission, rather than just another rehearsal band.

This was a large ensemble, even for a big band—five saxes, five trumpets, five trombones, piano, bass and drums—and when things got going, it was a freight train roaring right at you. I loved the feeling.

I had been a big band leader in high school and college. But the buzz I got from this one was more intense. Standing in front of it, experiencing the sheer power and energy, I knew I was meant to do to this—shape and guide this giant live music machine, which wouldn't exist without me. The band became my instrument.

Even in those early rehearsals we realized something unique was happening. We were creating a musical moment that excited us, made us feel alive, feel necessary, a reward of no small significance for musicians who were working at other jobs to make a living. Nothing more was needed to satisfy our love of big band jazz than to come together once a week, play new charts, improve our skills and recharge our spirits

After a year of rehearsing as a workshop group, and thoroughly enjoying the process, an unexpected situation developed. Duke Ellington wrote "I Got It Bad, And That Ain't Good." We had become good, and that could be bad.

The fun band evolved into something more serious, more polished. We paid attention to detail, rehearsed more intensely—not just running though arrangements and going on to the next. We cared about our sound. And as we raised our standards, the character of the band changed.

Ever more challenging arrangements had to be found to stimulate the musicians' desire to excel. Curiously, satisfying their growing desire for recognition became an even greater challenge. Rehearsals were rewarding, but that wasn't enough. Human nature being what it is, as the quality improved, the desire to perform our work imposed itself into our collective psyche. The 'boys' needed applause. Of course I could well understand that. I had never been one to run from an audience.

We discussed the situation and agreed. Although we were a big band rehearsal workshop, we would prepare for a public concert, charge admission, and see what happened. The goal refocused us.

Our first concert was to be a cultural event, so I was able to rent Central High School's 1500 seat auditorium from the Board of Education for $75.00. We presented it in the summer of 1958 with an expanded group—five saxes, four trombones, five trumpets and a double rhythm section, twenty of us in all. Ensuring our chances of success, I hired well-known jazz names as guests artists, "Zoot and Al" – Zoot Sims and Al Cohn, two of the finest saxophonists in jazz.

The concert was a sell-out and its success immediately established our prestige in the community. In time our concerts featured other famous jazz musicians as guest artists. We dropped the name Modern Music Workshop and became popularly known as the Jazz Giants.

We were filling a void, not only for ourselves, but also for thousands of people in the area who loved big band jazz, which was fading in popularity and no longer accessible on a regular basis. Although it took so much of my time, and I wasn't making much money with it, the effort to keep the *Jazz Giants* growing was extremely rewarding.

Once a week we rehearsed at Bill's Castle, a friendly, worn, neighborhood bar and sometime restaurant on Route 1-A. On Friday and Saturday nights, however, dinner was served in the adjoining dining room with white linens and generous portions of ownership pride. Bill, the owner, helped serve the home cooked food himself. Truck driver food, I called it—mashed potatoes and gravy, soups, steaks, ham, roast pork, corned beef and cabbage, and a few delicious Hungarian specialty dishes. He wore a long white butcher's apron and chatted with everyone who came into the place.

The façade of the building was white stucco. A garish, red neon sign, suspended in the bar window facing the street, spelled out *Bill's Castle* in script. Inside, opposite the rather dimly lit, long, clean bar, a row of hardwood tables and chairs neatly lined the wall. The adjoining dining room, unused during the week, had seen better days, but it had a dance floor and a small stage at one end. It was a fine place to rehearse a big band.

When I first met Bill I proposed that we rehearse free in his dining room on Wednesday nights. "It'll be good for your business, Bill. And it won't cost you anything."

A week later he said, "Well, we'll give it a try for a few weeks and see what happens."

We were still there after three years. Friends and fans dropped in to hear us. They'd buy a few drinks and liven up the atmosphere. It became a cheap place to go for the jazz cognoscenti in town. It was good for Bill and good for us.

The Musicians Union office called me one day and said they knew we were playing for free and that we would have to be paid or stop playing there.

"But we're just rehearsing," I said.

They didn't care. "Sorry. Drinks are served. No pay, no play." They were serious, and they had power to fine me if I didn't comply. Finding a place to rehearse a band that size wasn't easy. Since I hadn't had much love for the union before, this incident didn't exactly raise my barometer of goodwill. They just didn't get it. We were simply trying to make music.

So I made out a contract to Bill's Castle for $500 as "Fee for Services," i.e., public rehearsals. Then Bill made out an invoice to me labeled "Rehearsal Hall Rental – $500."

Each week I sent both signed papers to the union office.

There wasn't much they could do about it, and soon they stopped bothering me. But their interference reminded me that the Musicians Union, at least this one then, wasn't about helping musicians create music, but about rules and control.

As the band built a quality reputation in the region, we played more well-attended concerts and colleges dances, averaging about three dates a month, We had developed a creative, professional product that deserved to be more widely recognized. I poured all my energies into the Giants, probably giving it more than I should have, given I was still working full time at WICC and WJZZ-FM Radio. I often wonder now why I didn't just enjoy it and stop pushing? But I just couldn't. I was an alpha with a dream—a classic obsessive-compulsive combination. I kept hoping that maybe the Jazz Giants would turn into my big break-though.

We had been together for three years when we hit another critical impasse: boredom. This is a killer for musicians, who, once so afflicted, begin to find fault with everything. Rehearsals started turning into U.N. meetings.

"How much does the next job pay?" one of them said.

"I can't make rehearsal next week. Too busy," said another.

"How far do we have to drive to the gig?"

"My wife says I'm spending too much time doing this."

"Why are we playing there?"

"What are we playing this chart for?"

The natives were restless. We needed an incentive, a new goal, an inspiration, something important, something big, perhaps some kind of event. Day and night I thought about the band. How could I keep it moving forward? How could I boost us over the wall?

Every week I drove from Bridgeport to New York to talk to the best arrangers, looking for that special chart that would take us "up front" and be noticed. I met with agents, managers, promoters, venue owners and record companies. I sent out brochures, flyers, letters, copies of newspaper reviews, demo tapes and pictures. Still nothing. It all came down to recordings. Without a record, promoters wouldn't touch us. Record companies were simply not investing in unknown big jazz bands any more. Even Count Basie, one of the most famous big band leaders, was working with an eight-piece band for a while. Times were changing.

After almost four years of effort, we were on the verge of fizzling out. The band had to keep growing or it would assuredly fade away. I didn't want that to happen. I needed the Jazz Giants. I had to find a way to break through with them.

Then it hit me. What's the most prestigious jazz event? I kept coming back to the same answer. There was only one: the

GENE HULL

Newport Jazz Festival, known worldwide, the father of all jazz festivals. The 'World Series' of jazz. The biggest names played it. And every year it produced a best-selling record album of its concerts. As out of reach as it was, I decided to go for it. If the band was going to survive, I didn't feel I had much choice.

The line to get to George Wein, the Festival's producer, was, figuratively speaking, a mile long. Hundreds of bands wanted in. Without entree it was hopeless. Promotional mail and letters I sent to the Festival office were returned unopened. My calls were un-returned. I talked it up to everyone I knew in the business in New York. No one could offer any advice except, "You've got to get to George Wein." But there seemed to be no way.

Then fate stepped in. A few years before, I met Bob Messinger at a record session for Columbia Records in New York, where I was recording a flute piece I had written. He was in the booth during the recording session and liked the sound. We chatted afterwards and hit it off. Two months later Columbia released the tune, "Pico Peak-A-Boo"—named after Pico Peak in Vermont—on a 45 rpm with a promotional bio of me on the jacket.

Bob was a likeable, fast-talking, street-smart guy of thirty-five, who had radio station and record distributor contacts. He knew the business of record promotion and knew how to get airplay without paying for it. It was the days of rampant payola without which records didn't move. I couldn't pay him, but Bob offered to help.

A few weeks later "Pico Peak-a-Boo" came out at number 'Twenty with a Bullet' on the Billboard Top 100 chart, which meant that record stores should watch for it to break out. It got some national airplay, sold a few records, got mild acceptance in record outlets, and then faded to the returns bin. Bob had done all he could. The record died of natural causes, and, I liked to think, lack of payola. But in retrospect, it probably wasn't good enough to have a life of its own after initial exposure in the marketplace. I didn't expect much. It was more like a musical aside, so I wasn't crushed.

Things happen for a reason. Two years after that I recalled that Bob had said he worked as stage manager for George Wein each year at the Newport Festival. It was a long-shot, but why not talk to Bob, I thought? He had moved from New York, but I managed to trace him to a small, quiet town in northern New Jersey. He had quit the record promotion business, married, had a huge dog, and was writing a sports column for the local newspaper. "You still work the Newport Jazz Festival for George Wein?" I asked when I called.

"Sure. Every year," he said.

I told him all about how the Jazz Giants had grown. I asked if he would suggest to George Wein that we play the Festival that year. He laughed and said, "You gotta be kidding. Get in line. George even turned down Stan Kenton this year."

"I'm serious. Bob," I assured him. "We're good. The band swings. So it's not Kenton. But it's fresh. It's strong. You'd be a hero. Besides, we wouldn't cost nearly as much as Kenton. And we're practically in Newport's backyard."

Probably sensing some logic and certainly the passion in my voice, he said, "Well, send me some stuff and let me look at it. I'll see what I can do."

A week or so later, after I sent him all the promotional material I had, plus pictures and a reel tape of our concerts, he called and said, "Hey, I like it. The band is really good. I'm coming up to Connecticut to see a rehearsal." He came a week later. I didn't say anything to the guys; he watched and listened in the background.

After rehearsal he and I discussed possibilities. "Look, Gene, the band is exciting. But you have to understand that Newport is really a long shot. So please don't plan on anything. However, I do have an idea that might hold some air."

"What do you mean?"

"Every year George books one act for the Festival that's an unknown. You know, he likes to present it as a discovery. It's good for the Festival. Maybe he could see a connection in that way with the Jazz Giants. It might be a story he'd buy into, get promotional mileage out of it. And you said so yourself, you're right in Newport's back yard. How does this sound? 'Undiscovered New England Territory Jazz Big Band Plays the Famous Newport Jazz Festival in the Heart of New England.' "

"How about... 'Brilliant, undiscovered New England Territory Big Band'...."

"Yeah, sure," Bob chuckled. "George hasn't announced the lineup for the Festival yet. I'll ask him next week when I'm in his office. But remember, Gene, it's a long-shot."

"Why don't you call him now? Next week might be too late."

"It won't mean anything until he hears the tape. Be patient."

Be patient? Sure. Easy for you to say. This could be the breakthrough, the exposure, the record deal. It could change my life. I couldn't sleep. Long-shot or not, I was already counting on it and began visualizing playing on the Newport stage, though I'd never seen it.

One night at rehearsal, just before we called it a night, and the place pretty well emptied out, I said, "Guys, what would you think if we got booked to play at the Newport Jazz Festival this year?"

"Yeah sure, and the World Series, while we're at it," said Joe Daddona, our affable, sometimes acerbic, baritone sax player, a school teacher who had played in several name bands.

"How about Carnegie Hall?" called out Bobby Butler, an insurance adjuster by day, and our excellent lead trumpet man— we had actually played Carnegie Hall together in Roddy Shull's band when we were sixteen, placing second in *Look Magazine's*

National Swing Band contest. Most of the guys laughed and made comments like,

"Any time."

"Newport? Sure, why not?"

"Carnegie Hall."

"The White House."

"Hollywood, here we come."

"Guys, I'm dead serious," I said. "If I could get us booked to play at Newport this coming July, would you all be willing to double up on rehearsals to prepare for it? That's only five months away, and we'd have a ways to go. If we can pull it off, we'd want to be absolutely slick and stone everybody with our music."

"Gene, I don't know if you can really do this," drawled laconic Jack Spake, our North Carolina, jazz-chair trombonist. "But hell, if you can, I for one would work my tired old Southern butt off to see it happen." Lanky Jack was an easy-going, disheveled-looking, ex-GI, a good ole boy, who had been a trombonist in the U.S. Army Band. His slow, easy delivery kept you waiting for the next word to come out—it was usually worth the wait. He was a true gentleman, and the guys respected him.

"Whoa. I don't know if you're pulling our leg or not," said Joe Marzulli, "but remember, we're just a local Bridgeport rehearsal band." Outwardly gruff, Joe was really a sensitive guy, a budding arranger, a trumpeter and a fine high school band director.

"Newport is big time," he said. "That's a lot of pressure to put on us. Do we want that, guys?"

I didn't wait for anyone else's opinion. "This is what I think. Each year George Wein, the Festival's producer, presents one unknown jazz group along with his usual array of famous jazz stars."

"Yeah, so?" said Joe.

"The 'unknowns' are from anywhere in the world." I said. "Remember last year? It was the Wreakers from Poland? And the year before, the International Youth Band? They were presented as being fresh and new on the scene, and they wound up with record deals. It could be the same sort of opportunity for us. Besides, wouldn't it be fun just to see if we could pull it off? We're good, and you all know it. So why not?"

"But what's the point of wasting time trying for that if we don't get invited?" said saxophonist Ronnie Gebeau.

"The point is this. Why couldn't it be us? Why couldn't we be this year's Newport 'discovery?' We're pretty special. Hell, I've been waiting to be discovered since I was ten years old."

"Me too," said Mickey Walker, our lead jazz trombonist. "Me want fame. Fame mean money. Money make wife happy. Happy wife mean... well, you know... Ungawah!"

Everyone broke up. "Are you kidding? I'm up for it. It'd be great... and don't ever tell my wife I said that."

Dom Mariconda, another high school band director and trumpeter, who later became Superintendent of Music for Bridgeport Public Schools, said, "Gene, are you just spinning our wheels? Do you even know George Wein?"

"No, I don't. But I've got an idea, and I'm working on it. It could happen. If you guys are willing to commit the time for extra rehearsals, I'll go for it."

"Yeah, sure, fine," was their off-handed response. To most of them the idea was a pipe dream. And that was understandable. You get all worked up about something and then it doesn't happen, and you're left to deal with the disappointment and rejection. It happens a lot in this business. You pump yourself up because of something somebody says they're going to do for you, then... zilch! These guys just didn't want to set themselves up for a fall.

Even though I was sure they wouldn't even bother telling their wives or girlfriends there was a possibility they might be rehearsing more than one night a week, I knew they would be thrilled if it happened.

Bob Messinger called two weeks later. "George loves the idea. He buys the story. He'd like to do it."

"Fantastic! Incredible! He won't be disappointed."

"HOWEVER, the cost of a big band that size would be heavy for him. And you guys don't exactly have the kind of known name that draws an audience. He figures he'll lose too much money if he books you. Budgets are very tight this year."

"Does that mean no?"

"Probably. BUT... suppose you guys could sell a few tickets to the festival, if you are booked. You know, to help George offset some of his costs."

"Yeah, then what?"

"THEN... I think we can make a deal with him."

"You're serious?"

"Yep."

"How much in 'costs' do we have to offset?"

"One thousand dollars in tickets."

"How many tickets is that?"

"Less than two hundred at $5.40 each."

It sounded fair to me. "Deal. Let's do it. Send me the contract."

"You sure?"

"Are you kidding? Absolutely."

So we made the deal. I committed to selling about two hundred $5.40 tickets. I figured we could unload those easily at our local concerts. Besides, we had over 800 names on our mailing list and months to go before the Festival.

It was done. It was going to happen. I couldn't believe it. No dream. It was the Big League. I couldn't wait to share the news with the band. They surely would be as ecstatic as I was. But it didn't turn out that way.

A possible Newport performance would be a moment of truth for them—'sink or swim.' The reality of it caught them by surprise, sobered them. They had doubts. Were we really good at just the local level? Would we be credible on the national scene, or maybe a joke?

We had another hurdle to get over.

*

So, nothing is easy. You asked for it. Don't expect any sympathy from me. Remember, Confucius say:

*"Man who reach up for star.
sometime not see bump on road."*

(Oh, give me a break. You're worse than I am. Are you sure you're me?)

Heh, heh.

**

Thirteen

THE NEWPORT JAZZ FESTIVAL

It was official. The Jazz Giants would perform at the 1962 Newport Jazz Festival, the world's most prestigious jazz event. Bridgeport people would hardly believe it. Nor would the musicians; they'd celebrate. But something strange happened when I told the band a deal had been made. I expected a roar of excitement and maybe some applause. Instead they were quiet. Too quiet. I could see an uneasy look on their faces.

"Aw, man, I don't know," said one.

"You serious?" another said. A few grumbled. The rest looked down at their music, avoiding my eyes. Their reaction surprised me, confusing me at first. The whole deal would go sour if this was their true feeling. My first reaction was, *hey you guys, I put this thing together after we all agreed. Remember? Now you're telling me you don't want to do it?* But I didn't say that. It would either intimidate them into a weak, "Okay, we'll go," or the band would dissolve. Either way I'd lose. I tried to understand their obstinacy. Had I moved too fast? Was it really not a good thing for them? Or was it in fact 'put-up or shut-up' time and they didn't think it would ever come to this? Perhaps they were afraid to risk their local reputations on a world stage. Locally, we were important. But were we really as good as we thought? Or would the elite professional music world not take us seriously? By declining, there would be no risk.

Yes, that was it. I couldn't let the opportunity collapse because of their lack of confidence. I knew we were capable of doing ourselves a great deed, one they would be proud of for a long time. But if we were to succeed, the will to do it had to be unanimous. I decided to give it my best shot with a short impassioned speech. "Come on, guys, this is our chance. A golden opportunity to prove ourselves. We've worked hard for this. Believe in yourselves. You're good. We can do it. I know we can. We'd make a lot of people proud. I think we should go for it. But it's up to you."

With nothing left to say, I waited.

After a long silence, Jack Spake drawled, "Gene, I can't think of a better present than the one you just gave us. It's something I've only dreamed of. Now I can live it."

Jack's comments made the guys think. They pulled out of the negative slump. Chatter started. Doubt was shoved under chairs. Joe Daddona spoke up, "Right. So let's get to work, guys."

Suddenly we were a band with a purpose again. Their new resolve had cheated disaster. It was like a 1940's family movie - the old Mickey Rooney/Judy Garland musicals where the gang or club saves the day by 'putting on a show' in the barn. I guess clichés are based on fact.

I received the contract via Registered Mail. The first clause confirmed we were to open the show on Saturday night, July 7th, with a forty-five minute set. We had not been relegated to some afternoon workshop, which could have happened. This was a prime-time spot. Wow. Bob Messinger, I love you.

The next clause stated we would sell about two hundred $5.40 tickets, which would be sent to us. Fine. Right. But then it went on to say that the $1,000 for the tickets was to be remitted in advance to the Festival office, together with the signed contract, within seven days, or the contract would be null and void. What? A thousand dollars! I can't believe it. Can't be.

I didn't have a thousand dollars, and had no idea where to get it. In 1962 that kind of money was more like ten thousand in today's times. My wife and I had recently bought a house. Mortgage payments took some doing with seven kids by then. No money, no contract. No way the deal can happen now.

I made several inquiries, not mentioning the 'snafu' to the guys. It might burst their bubble. This issue was about money, not music. I wanted them to stay focused.

By the fifth day I was out of ideas. I could feel Newport slipping away. I had already announced to everyone that we were going. After coming so close, I hurt. I was embarrassed, depressed, even morose. I went to see my friend and family doctor, Mike Cardone, Chief of Staff at St. Vincent's Hospital who had delivered most of my seven kids. (Our eighth was born soon after.) Mike was married to Betty Jane, my first cousin.

He listened to the whole story and calmed me down. "Gene, let me talk to some of the guys in the band...our band."

Ironically, Dr. Mike played baritone sax in the Doctors' Big Band. They met every few weeks for fun, to unwind, play a few tunes, drink a few scotches and talk about music and the good old days. Strictly an amateur group, I coached them whenever they rehearsed. It never occurred to me to ask them for help. Dr. Mike called that night. "Don't worry, Gene, we'll put up the grand. Pay us back when you sell the tickets. You've done a lot for us. So go, man."

GENE HULL

There was a Santa Claus after all. I'll never forget the relief I felt. And I'll never forget Dr. Mike. Without him, Eddie Kochan, Marv Aaron and Bob Gaffney of the 'Doctors Big Band,' Newport would not have happened for us. The next day I sent out the signed contracts and a cashier's check for $1,000. The tickets arrived by return mail. We were going!

Months zoomed by with extra rehearsals, arrangements being polished, new ones written, PR mailings to hundreds of jazz fans, stories and interviews in local papers, even radio interviews. Interest in us steamrolled. We were becoming a household name in Connecticut. The Bridgeport Herald did a full-page spread with pictures of the 'Jazz Giants in rehearsal preparing for the Big Day,' as did the Bridgeport Post, and Hartford and New Haven papers later. I continued to work full time at the radio station, and they were most understanding of the time I gave to this project.

I had met U.S. Congressman Don Irwin, while covering his re-election bid for WICC Radio. He was an avid jazz fan and a Jazz Giants supporter who wrote a "Jazz Giants Salute Proclamation Letter" to the papers. On the weekend of our performance he led an auto caravan of fans to Newport, about a hundred and twenty miles distant.

Finally, the Fourth of July weekend arrived, Newport weekend. We had done everything I could think of to prepare. We were ready. The morning of our evening show, we warmed up, playing a few tunes, getting loose, in a small local Newport bar, a dank, neighborhood joint, which resourceful Bob Messinger had found for us. The smell of stale beer permeated the place as it does most beer joints before they open for business. We didn't mind; we were used to it from Bill's Castle —and Bill's *was* a castle compared to this place. It was the dark kind of bar where, when you bravely step out into daylight after hours inside, the sun splash makes your couple of beers feel like five.

At eleven o'clock in the morning it was packed with friends, wives, insiders and touted press who wanted to catch a preview of the 'Band from Bridgeport.' As we finished, Bob came bouncing in telling me that Russell Procope was ill and wouldn't be able to play with Duke Ellington's band the following night.

Remembering that I had subbed with Ellington before for Johnny Hodges and Procope, he asked if I wanted to play with the band for their Sunday night show.

"You kidding? Twist my arm." Good things come in bunches. Incredible.

At that point I happened to reach into my pocket and found sixty tickets. I realized we hadn't sold all of them. Oops. I had been too busy with all our preparations. I flipped them out and flashed them like a deck of cards. "Ladies," I said, "can you take care of these?"

"Come on, girls," said Joyce D'Addario, wife of Pete D'Addario, our dynamic drummer, an alumnus of the Sauter-Finegan Orchestra, and owner of a local Bridgeport music store. "Lets go to work." And they did.

Two hours before show time the wives and girl friends of the band spread out between the huge parking lot and the entrance gate, hawking tickets. I don't know if George Wein was ever aware of that scene, but the women sold all the remaining tickets in twenty minutes. We were family.

We kicked off our program at 8:00 PM. I don't remember a note we played; it went so fast. But I do remember the brass section screaming out into the night with colossal fire. The saxes steamed together like bonded brothers and took their ensemble sound to another level. From our first note, the energy and drive poured over me, almost putting me in a trance. The band was like a locomotive. Get out of the way everybody. Here we come.

The applause was generous from the sell-out crowd who had come expecting to see the famous. Joe Marzulli had written an original composition, which he called "Little Big Horn." He didn't think it was good enough to play there, but it was, and we did. And it was a hit. Trumpeter Dom Mariconda's solo was vibrant. Bobby Butler, one of our two lead trumpets, played brilliantly. As did Mickey Walker. So did saxophonist soloists Ronnie Gebeau, Dick Burlant, Al Provenzano and Steve Royal, who later toured with Woody Herman's band. Dick Burlant, Tony Guzzi and Russ Martino had written some fine arrangements. In reality, most every player had managed to play close to his best at the same time. A rare moment for us. I was proud to stand up there in front of this real band of brothers, who had laid it out for all to hear. *This is who we are, world.*

Also on the program that night were Charlie Mingus, Toshiko Mariano, the Max Roach Quartet and Louis Armstrong and his All Stars. From Louis, who watched us backstage from the wings, I could hear loud encouraging grunts of 'Uh huh's,' whenever something we played particularly pleased him. Audience reception was even more enthusiastic than we had hoped. Famous musicians came up to us later with congratulations. The dream was finally coming true. We were climbing onto the ole' "Cloud Nine". Most importantly, we had delivered our best to ourselves. I was proud of everyone.

Our celebration afterwards was ardent, to say the least. We partied till almost dawn. We had done it. We had gotten the attention of the Jazz world, the press, music critics and important venue operators. The buzz was genuine. Best of all, the whole Newport four-day event was recorded by Impulse Records. We would finally have a recording as one of the Festival's acts. No band could be taken seriously without a record. Our teamwork and efforts had paid off.

The band and our entourage of a hundred people or more had stayed Friday and Saturday nights at Newport's Seaview Motel, where we had reserved the entire first floor. Even so, there weren't enough rooms. In some cases we had eight people to a room, crashing wherever they could find space.

At ten Sunday morning the word went around the motel. "Everybody up!" Father Fred, a long time friend and fan, who made the trip with us, arranged to say 11 o'clock Mass in honor of the *Jazz Giants* at a nearby parish Church. Most of us (those who could still walk) attended, no matter what religion or non-religion we professed. It was a brilliant morning—squinting was the alternative to snow blindness. We could hardly keep the sand out of our eyes. From the moans and groans, I knew some heads were pounding, as if a jungle percussion section were playing inside them.

Father Fred Trumbull had been a handsome, dark-haired, popular Central High School football quarterback in Bridgeport, though he was only 5' 6' and 140 pounds. He also was a talented singer and had won local "Frank Sinatra" contests at the Loew's Theatre when he was a student, as well as singing with my high school band before going into the U.S. Army. Upon his discharge, he enrolled in a seminary, became a priest, and had just returned from eight years as a missionary in Tanganyika, where he had built a hospital. We all loved him.

Midway though the Mass, the local pastor turned to the congregation and made a simple announcement. "Today's sermon will be given by a visiting missionary priest, who has just returned from the missions in Central Africa, Father Fred Trumbull, from the Holy Ghost Order."

There were expectant murmurs from the regular parishioners, who were well aware, I'm sure, of the bleary-eyed strangers uncharacteristically filling the church on this hot, July Sunday morning. There was a respectful silence as Father Fred stepped up into the pulpit. They were expecting, I'm sure, to hear about the African Missions and possibly an appeal for financial support. After all, he was the out-of-town expert on mission matters, and missions always needed money. As for our contingent, we perked up to hear 'our guy.' After all, he had partied with us most of the night. We felt special, as he cleared his throat.

"Good morning, everyone. Ahem." He began, with the serious tone of an important Church dignitary about to share with the faithful the story of the woes and challenges of the African Missions.

"Thank you, Pastor Kiernan, for inviting me to help celebrate Mass here today. Ahem. In deference to those who have labored long and hard through the night, yet have had the strength of character to arise this hot morning and come to this lovely church to give thanks, today's sermon will be short. Go in peace. Love one another. God bless you all. Thank you."

Winking at us, he stepped down from the pulpit. It was, I'm sure, the shortest sermon on record at St. Mary's Church.

Afterward, we all had a picnic lunch together. "Brevity is next to Deity," said Father Fred with a twinkle, as he sipped a welcome orange juice.

Sunday night I played with the Duke Ellington Orchestra. The park had opened at seven for the eight o'clock show. Thousands of people were finding their seats as the Ellington band members straggled onto the stage, one by one, for a pre-show rehearsal. I was the first one on stage, anxious and ready to go. I noticed Cat Anderson, Duke's extraordinary lead trumpet player, amble onto the bandstand, sit down at his place, open up his trumpet case and pull out a comic book. He proceeded to place it on his music stand and 'read' with obvious amusement.

There was no curtain. We were in full view of the audience. It was starting to get dark. More musicians arrived. Then the great Thelonious Monk, jazz innovator of the first magnitude, strolled on stage. He received a hug from Duke and sat down at the piano. Monk was, well... Monk, in his tam and goatee, quiet, gentle, friendly as usual, with no need for mundane insincerities like publicly shaking hands. A wave to the musicians would do.

He pounded a few two-second, three-fingered dissonant chord clusters—Monk chords, I would guess—got up and walked off stage. He never came back. Because Duke's program ran long that night, Monk performed with him the following night.

Duke introduced Aretha Franklin, then an unknown, who sat in and played piano with the band for a few tunes. Aretha was only sixteen at the time and wore a frilly, lavender party dress. Her singing talents were yet to be discovered. Ten minutes before show time Duke started passing out parts while Billy Strayhorn was still writing a new arrangement that the band would play with Aretha on piano. I kept looking at my watch. When are we going to rehearse? This could be disastrous. But no one else seemed concerned.

Before we had time to play a note of the new charts, or even tune up, it was showtime. Talk about a band being relaxed! As if on automatic pilot, drummer Sam Woodyard kicked into a brief clip of Duke's "Take The 'A' Train" theme, then right into "Satin Doll." After that, Duke called out, "Rockin' In Rhythm, boys." Turning to the audience, he proceeded to deliver one of his famous, splendiferously warm and eloquent greetings, concluding with, "The boys in the band and I want you to know we all 'Love You Madly.' " Duke was grandly polite in greeting people, the way men and women of a different era often were. The crowd loved him.

Duke's music library was not numbered. Instead, the arrangements were placed in the musicians' folders alphabetically. There were well over a hundred of them. While he was speaking to the crowd, I opened to the R's, quickly searching for "Rockin' In Rhythm." None of the other saxophone players even bothered to look for music. Evidently they knew the chart by heart. I finally found "Rockin' In Rhythm," but there were four different arrangements of the same tune!

"Which chart?" I said in a panic to Harry Carney, who was seated beside me.

GENE HULL

He laughed a little, like it didn't make any difference, and said, "Man, just start on your high D and follow me." With that the entire sax section arose, Jimmy Hamilton, Johnny Hodges, Paul Gonzalves, Harry Carney and I. We left our places, and grouped downstage around the mike. Baritone sax player Harry played clarinet on this particular arrangement, doubling the lead alto part exactly, only an octave higher. I played the alto melody by ear, just a fraction of a millisecond behind Harry with an ear glued to him. I fudged notes I wasn't sure of and laid it on strong where I was confident. Duke listened. I didn't get in the way. He was pleased and beamed his ear-to-ear smile.

Later in the program just about everyone in the band soloed a few choruses on an extended blues number, with Duke giving each soloist a grand introduction. "And now," he announced, as the band vamped, "the man whose band from Bridgeport broke it up last night here at Newport, Mr. Gene Hull."

I really don't remember playing the solo. It couldn't have made much sense. I was exhausted by then. The adrenaline that had driven me for the past several months seeped out my seams. I was fading. Late that night my wife, a friend and I drove back to Connecticut. I fell asleep in the backseat and awoke a few hours later as the car pulled into the driveway of our home.

The sense of accomplishment I felt was worth everything it had taken to do it. After all, the *Jazz Giants* had finally been recorded, and the album would get worldwide distribution. We had finally gotten over the hump.

For weeks we basked in the acclaim. New England papers gave it a big play. The New York Herald Tribune did a glowing article about us, as did the New York Times. Dave Brubeck wrote, "...the best thing to happen to the Newport Jazz Festival." The City of Bridgeport was demonstrably proud. I was asked to join the City Arts Council. The University of Notre Dame Magazine later did a full-page spread with a picture of the band. A white cloth banner – "HOME of the JAZZ GIANTS"—

hung at Bill's Castle. I even got an extension on my bank loan. A minor miracle. Ah, the glory of it all! The $1,000 was repaid to the doctors. Our band was filled with newborn pride.

A month later I got a call from Bob Messenger. "Gene, sit down. I have to tell you something."

"More good news, I hope. You've got a release date for the album?"

"Yeah, it turned out great. Wait till you hear it. Congratulations."

"Yeow!"

Six months later the album of Newport '62 was released featuring the 45-minute program of the Jazz Giants. It sold 500,000 albums worldwide the first year, a huge number for a jazz album. Our future was assured. Back up the truck for the money. I felt vindicated and immensely relieved. Opportunity had been met with preparation. The work, the hours, the planning, the rehearsing and the dedication had been worth it. Luck, the most precious requirement for success in the entertainment business, had smiled on us. Life was indeed good.

*

Oh really? So where's the recording?

(Ah, yes, that little detail, the recording. Okay, the story didn't end in glory. I was just wishing.)

That's why I'm here.

A month later I got a call from Bob Messenger. "Gene, sit down. I have to tell you something."

"More good news, I hope. You've got a release date for the album?"

"No, I'm afraid not,' he said. "All of the tapes from the Festival were spoiled by some electronic quirk during the live recording at Newport."

"What? Are you kidding me, man?"

"No one heard it during the tapings in the sound truck, but back here in New York, in the studio mixing session, it's obvious that all the tapes are defective."

"What does that mean, Bob? No Jazz Giants tape? No recording? No album?"

"No recordings of the entire 1962 Newport Jazz Festival! There will be no Festival album this year. It's never happened before. It's a huge blow to George."

"Yeah, I can appreciate that," I said quietly. "Tell him I'm sorry for his bad luck."

"You okay, Gene?"

"Wanna buy a saxophone?" I said in utter disbelief, crushed.

"I'm sorry," he said.

"Me, too." What else was there to say?

"But I do have you booked to play alternate Monday nights at Birdland this summer," Bob said.

"With my luck it'll probably close before we get there."

"Gene, did you hear me? Birdland. Broadway and 52nd Street, 'The Jazz Corner of he World.' It's the most famous jazz club on the planet."

"Yes, I know."

Many bands didn't last as long. We had more than our "fifteen minutes"—eight years in all. Birdland didn't close; we carried the sounds of our music to the Big Apple that summer and the next. It was a special treat. Many famous musicians came to hear us. Years of many fine moments followed, performing with movie stars, famous singers, celebrities, and jazz personalities, such as Jack Benny, Bob Hope, Mel Torme, Doc Severinson, Sammy Davis, Tony Bennett, The Four Tops, Gloria DeHaven, Dave Brubeck, Art Blakey, Neil Sedaka, Urbie Green, Sonny Stitt, Rosemary Clooney, Bill Evans and countless others. We had more than our share of fun, fame and glory. I feel we created some extraordinary notes in time. But ultimately the Jazz Giants were lost in memory with no 'recorded' history, a big band dinosaur extinct before its time.

**

Fourteen

LENNIE

"Daddy, the kitten has six toes on its back feet."

"Really? Count 'em again, sweetheart. Cats paws usually have five toes."

"I know that," Becky, our five-year old daughter said. "Look," holding the gangly kitten up to me. "See? One, two, three, four, five, six."

"Well, I'll be. You're right, a cat with twenty-two toes. Whadaya know."

"Please, please, please. Can we keep him, Daddy? please," Amy said.

"Please Dad," the others chimed in.

The straggly gray kitten had surprised me that morning, crawling out from under the front seat as I unloaded the band's music and stands from the car. Apparently, the night before it had hidden in the car at Bill's Castle while I was packing up after an evening rehearsal. There were a couple of stray cats nearby at the time. I was amazed to find him now. He stretched, looked around and yawned. He was a plain, skinny, alley-variety stray, most likely separated from his mother. When I picked him up he gave me a curious, almost blasé expression that seemed to say, "Okay, I'm here. So what do we do now?" I laughed. He must have been frightened, but he wasn't a bit intimidated. I liked his spunk.

I was not a cat lover, anything but. Our pets were always dogs. Up until that time I had always regarded cats as being of no consequence. After all, if they weren't dogs, it was difficult to think of them as man's best friend. But something about this kitten was different. I immediately felt responsible for him, perhaps struck by his personality and air of independence. Yet there was nothing capricious about him.

Willingly, I believe, he joined in with the family flow. The kids took him everywhere. Cyrano, our brown and white Sheltie, a family member for several years, often sleeping sprawled out and content on the floor, tolerated the kitten's impromptu surprise attacks with adult-like forbearance. The kitten loved to play anytime; he wasn't shy or coy. He wouldn't have survived if he were. A family of eight energetic children is not the place for anyone shy, especially a pet.

Weeks passed. The kitten grew but strangely, remained unnamed. The kids could not agree on what to call him. It was that kind of a family. All had their own favorite name: Cuddles, Tiger, Mouser, Pussy, Lion, Bitty Kitty, Honey, Killer, Fang, Big Foot, Rabbit, etc. I referred to him as Jazz Giant Cat. After all, it was after a Jazz Giants rehearsal that the kitten had stowed away in my car and come into our lives.

One day the appropriate name seemed to strike the whole family at the same time. It was obvious. There could be no other name. It was solved. Everyone agreed. As bubbly and crazy as he was at times, bounding over furniture, friends and fences, as if possessed, the cat had a more curious and most distinctive habit—unlike any animal I have ever known.

At that time, we were in the habit of watching the Leonard Bernstein's "Young People's Concerts with the New York Philharmonic" telecasts live on Saturdays. He demonstrated the sounds of various instruments, and in his mellifluous tones, rich, deep and pleasant, he told stories about the music and composers. The family loved the program. We'd gather in the living room, settling on couches or sprawling out on the carpet in front of the Philco console black and white TV.

But it wasn't just the children who enjoyed Leonard Bernstein and the music. The cat watched too, and right next to the screen. Whenever there was a close-up of Bernstein, speaking into the camera, the cat would get closer to the TV screen and focus wide-eyed on his every movement. If he raised his hand or gestured or nodded, the cat was right with him. Clearly the cat was fascinated.

On the day Bernstein narrated *Peter and the Wolf*, the cat was particularly transfixed. His appreciation took on a new manifestation. Nodding and dipping, he began to follow Bernstein's hand and baton all around the screen, back and forth. The cat was one with Bernstein. That's all it took.

Some of the kids huddled then swarmed around us. "Mom! Dad! We've got the name, the cat's name. It's perfect."

"It's Leonard Catstein," said Matthew, matter-of-factly. And so it was. We all laughed. What could be more fitting for a cat who loved the Philharmonic's famous conductor? From that day, we called him Leonard Catstein. When the girls scolded him for stealing a sock or swiping a toothbrush, they called him Leonard, as in "LEONARD, you naughty kitty, come back here with that sock right now!" The boys sometime called him Lennie. But of course we always introduced him to our friends by his full proper name.

Ironically, the following summer, 1963, the Jazz Giants band was invited to play a concert at the home of Leonard Bernstein in Fairfield, Connecticut for a Sunday afternoon

Norwalk NAACP benefit. Several well-known jazz artists including the Billy Taylor Trio, Morgana King and Dizzy Gillespie were also performing.

The stage was set up on a gently sloped, tree-surrounded lawn not far from his large white clapboard, brick-chimneyed country house. Several hundred people attended, sportily accoutered in typical Fairfield County dressy-casual attire appropriate for a garden event. A few hundred chairs were set up on the lawn. It was a beautiful, clear, crisp August afternoon. Smells of grass and flowers scented the air; trees were peppered with an audience of feathered chirpers. An idyllic setting.

Between acts the audience mixed and mingled, had cocktails, and generally socialized. Bernstein was an affable host, shaking hands and chatting with many friends. It was an informal, yet elegant, day.

The *Jazz Giants* performed a fifty-minute program and were warmly received. Near the end of our time, I went to the microphone and thanked Mr. Bernstein for inviting us. Then, before introducing a jazz version of "Something's Coming" from Bernstein's *West Side Story*, I decided to chat a bit with the audience. I told them the story of a little stray, twenty-two-toed kitten that had lived in an alley behind the nightclub where the Jazz Giants rehearsed, and how he had hidden in my car one night.

I noticed Bernstein, standing in back, break away from a conversation in order to listen. I went on to tell how the kitten was truly fascinated by Mr. Bernstein's close-ups on television, and how as a result, the kids had named him 'Leonard Catstein,' or 'Lennie' for short. I thanked Mr. Bernstein for inspiring the name and for solving a family dilemma.

Bernstein seemed to enjoy the story. The crowd laughed and applauded. But in the audience, my mother shrank in embarrassment, even though it was the kind of relaxed, informal setting in which the story seemed appropriate... in my view at least.

Afterward, while I stood next to the bandstand greeting various 'patrons of the arts,' my mother (all four feet ten inches of her) approached me stern-faced. Usually smiling and congratulatory after one of our concerts, she waited until the people had trickled away from me, then scolded, "How could you tell that story, Gene? A cat, yet. It was rude and very disrespectful to Mr. Bernstein. You should know better than that." She thought the world of Bernstein, and was seriously displeased with me, probably for the first time in my life, that I can remember, though I really couldn't say for sure.

"Aw, come on Marge, it was all in fun. The crowd enjoyed it, and I'm sure Mr. Bernstein did too."

Suddenly Bernstein approached, appearing upset. "Listen. Buddy, why don't you take your cat and band and leave. This isn't a back alley with stray cats. This is my home. Who do you think you are?"

I was amazed at his indignation. I didn't know what to say. It was just a little fun, an entertaining story, I thought. Evidently, he didn't think so. He was nothing like he was on the children's TV concerts.

Marge looked at me. "See, I told you that was in bad taste." Facing Bernstein she said, "I'm so sorry, Mr. Bernstein. My son should have known better."

"Hmm," he said, turned and walked away.

I never watched the Philharmonic again after that, nor did my kids. As far as the cat was concerned, we started calling him Elvis.

*

*Cute. But I've got to say this now. 'Liar, liar, house on fire!'
Bernstein was a true gentleman. He would have never done that.*

(Jeez. I thought I'd just spice it up a bit. Okay, okay. Sorry, Mr. Bernstein. Actually, the conversation after the concert really went like this.)

"Aw, come on Marge, it was all in fun. The crowd enjoyed it and I'm sure Mr. Bernstein did too." Suddenly Bernstein approached, grinning.

"Yes I did, Gene," he said. " It was a fun story. I've never heard anything like that before. Does Lennie play piano too?" He chuckled. "I mean something besides "Kitten On The Keys?" He really amused himself with that one. The gravelly timbre of his voice sounded as if he just woke up.

I laughed at his pun.

My mother was jaw-slack speechless. HE was there. Bernstein HIMSELF.

"Mr. Bernstein, this is my mother, Marge," I said. "She really hates cats, but she loves you and you music." Which was true.

Warmly he shook her hand. "So nice to meet you, Mrs. Hull."

My mother gulped and gathered herself together in less time than it took to introduce her. With restored composure, her blue eyes twinkling, she gazed up at her idol, smiled sweetly and said "It's such an honor to meet you, Mr. Bernstein. Isn't my son wonderful?"

**

Fifteen

THE ICONS

Basie and Sarah

During the 60s I produced jazz concerts in the Connecticut area, probably more than a hundred in all. Many featured some of the world's best-known artists. On Monday nights, in conjunction with bassist/singer and energetic friend Dan Arcotta, I promoted a monthly Big Band series called "Cocktails and Concert," held in Bridgeport's Stratfield Hotel Ballroom.
    Tables were set up cabaret style, like Boston Pops presentations, with a modest admission price of $5.00, a cash bar and table service. We received the admissions and split the bar revenue, after costs, with the hotel. In turn we paid for the talent. We always sold out the room on those nights. It was successful for everyone. Things usually ran smoothly with no surprises, that is, until the night we presented Count Basie and his Orchestra. Every table was filled, every seat taken. As show time approached, the undercurrent buzz of the audience gathered momentum, not unlike like the excitement of a

grandstand crowd before the imminent start of a horse race. Basie had never played Bridgeport before in a concert setting. For local fans it was as if they were kids and the Beatles had come to town.

I was as excited as anyone. Basie was one of my favorites. Anticipation peaked, until finally it was show time. "Ladies and Gentlemen," I announced from the stage, "Welcome to another presentation of 'Cocktails and Concert.' I won't keep you waiting any longer. I know you're as anxious as I am to hear this great band. So here he is, The Kid from Redbank, Mr. Count Basie and his Orchestra." With that the marvelous Basie music machine, sixteen men swinging, began to roll, much to the delight of the overflow crowd.

They were indeed into it from the first note. Excitement spiraled as applause greeted each soloist—the audience clapping in time, whistling, and cheering the band with rapture. It was as if the audience were in the band, a spontaneous symbiotic bonding. These were the rare moments I lived for.

Count Basie was the kind of person who always seemed to know just where he was. A short, heavy set, friendly man, he had stuck with his band's uncomplicated, unique, driving style, because it was natural and fun and people loved it. He never seemed out to prove anything, except perhaps there could be no real big-band jazz without a solid, unified musical groove. As a result, his arrangements were relatively uncomplicated, conceptualized to let the band swing. And it did so with amazing impact. The ensemble sound he created was the era's standard for musical power and simplicity, a sound that could lift you and rock you and force you to feel alive. If his band didn't get to you, you were dead.

During intermission Sarah Vaughn approached me and asked if she could sing a few tunes with Basie. I hadn't realized she was in the audience. It seemed her sister lived in Bridgeport, and Sarah had just happened to come up from New York for a visit. I had recorded with her in the past, and I was surprised and delighted to see her. What a coup for our production... Sarah Vaughn, truly one of the greatest jazz singers ever, here at our presentation. Though a performer, I was capable of being as star-struck as the fans. And I was.

Up on stage I spoke to Basie just before the start of the second set. He was already seated at the piano. "Count, you sound ferociously terrific tonight," I said. "I've got a little surprise. Sarah is here and would like sit in with you and sing a few tunes." I tried to sound matter of fact about it, as if it were nothing unusual. But inside I was bubbling up like a circus clown. "Is that all right with you?"

"Sarah is here in Bridgeport?"

"Right. Her sister lives here."

"Hell yes, man. It'd be a ball. Where is she? I'll introduce her."

"Well, if you don't mind, I'd like to present her," I said. "You know, as a surprise guest star."

"Whoa, man. It's my band. I want to bring her on. You dig?"

"Sure, of course I do. But, Count, I'm the producer of the show. And it'd be really good for my business if I presented her. You understand, don't you?"

"She's never sung with my band here before, man. This is history. I'd like to introduce her."

I was surprised at his resistance. I knew he had a point, but so did I. I decided to give it one more try before caving in; after all, he was the star. "I'm sure she'll sing with you lots of times in the future, Count. Come on, this is only little old Bridgeport. Make me look good. You can have her next time. Okay?"

Basie gave me a knowing smile, cocked his head a little, seeming to acknowledge some internal voice of wisdom, and said, "I see, Gene. I get it. You want to be *the man*. You want to present Sarah. Okay. No problem. Go ahead."

I thanked him for his understanding, but I felt a little guilty as I went to the mike and made the announcement with as much pride and pomp as I could gather.

"Ladies and Gentlemen, it is our most happy pleasure to present tonight's special surprise guest star, the one, the only, THE DIVINE ONE, MISS SARAH VAUGHN!"

Basie, resplendent in his blue tuxedo, got up from the piano bench. Smiling at everyone, he crossed the stage, eased over to the wings and escorted Sarah on stage with great and gracious ceremony, as if he had rehearsed the whole scenario. Any static in the air between us dissolved immediately. The crowd was on its feet screaming with surprised delight. An unexpected delicious dessert was topping their musical feast.

Sarah sang beautifully with superb accompaniment from the Basie band. It was a rare moment indeed.

This incident may seem like much ado about nothing, certainly a minor incident in the course of a life. But it was important to me—a lesson learned. Bill 'Count' Basie was an exemplary bandleader; most everyone would agree. He consistently presented his finely disciplined swinging band with relaxed and confident aplomb to great effect. But in the subtle way of a wise gentleman, he demonstrated something else to me. By giving in he showed he was more 'the man' that night than I was.

Sir Duke

Of all the dynamic people in the entertainment world Duke Ellington stands out to me like no other. He was in a class by himself. Elegant, yet down to earth. Famous the world over, yet unaffected. A strong leader, yet gentle and gentlemanly.

Exceedingly bright, yet unpretentious. Patient, warm, considerate. Over the years he always regarded his marvelously talented band members as people first, musicians second. How unlike many high achievers in the music business.

Always in control, Duke had an insouciant air about him—gracious and urbane, witty in a friendly way with an interesting sense of humor. During intermission at one of our presentations, he signed autographs on several ladies girdles, after they had giddily hiked up their skirts for him. "Charmed, dahling," he said to each with debonair grace.

"I'm never washing this again," I heard more than one young woman say.

I had played in his band a few times over the years as a substitute saxophonist on occasions when Russell Procope or Johnny Hodges, his two regular alto saxophonists, were unavailable. And again at the 1962 Newport Jazz Festival. I had also recorded with him some time before in Chicago on a session which featured Betty Roche singing "Love You Madly." Years later I was to produce him in our 'Cocktails and Concert' series. In all that time I had never once seen him angry or outwardly upset, yet he remained a true artist, an exemplary band leader.

He was known for his habit of not reacting when provoked. His philosophy was that reactive knee-jerking just caused him pain. As a result, he wouldn't let himself become needlessly agitated. It was often said he refused to be drawn into any kind of verbal confrontation. I once witnessed an example of this first hand.

Duke had done excellent business for us when we presented him in our 'Cocktails and Concert' show in Bridgeport. The following month we presented him in Meriden, Connecticut, in the ballroom of the Holiday Inn in the same format.

On the day of the concert, by the time I got to Meriden at five in the afternoon to help get things organized, the band had already set up for the eight o'clock show.

As I hurried through the door, an agitated Joe Sully, Duke's road manager, greeted me with. "Gene, can you please do something about that radio station guy? He's been talking to Duke for forty-five minutes now. He's being rude and insulting."

"What radio guy?" I said.

Apparently a local radio representative was interviewing Duke with a Wollensak tape recorder in the cocktail lounge.

"They're over there in that booth," said Sully. "He just asked Duke how it feels 'to be a black man in a white man's world?' He's deliberately trying to provoke him. "

"What?" I said. "Let me at him."

After listening to the interview for just a few moments. I saw red. The guy was a complete ass.

"Do you find white women attractive, Duke?" he said.

"Do you?" Duke responded politely.

I was totally embarrassed. Worse, I felt responsible that some twerp was belittling one of the world's greatest musicians of all time. Duke gently parried with the man—who in my view deserved a smack—all the while maintaining his composure. You would never have known from Duke's demeanor that the radio guy was an offensive lout.

Finally, it had gone far enough. "Excuse me," I said, looking the interviewer in the eye. "Who are you anyway?"

"I'm the local radio D.J. on the morning show. "

"I don't recognize you. What station?" I said.

"The Meriden one." I knew everyone at the station. He wasn't on the pass list.

"Let me see your ID and press pass," I said.

"Who are you?" he challenged.

"I'm the producer and you are not authorized to be here. What do you think you're doing?"

"Oh man, I'm not really in radio," he said with a sheepish grin, as if caught with his hand in the cook jar. "But I love to get celebrities on tape. It's my hobby," offering this lame excuse, like it should make a difference.

"Give me the tape and get the hell out of here," I said. "And NOW."

When he had left, I turned to Duke, feeling like two cents. Make it one. "I am so sorry, Duke," I said. "That should never have happened. I'm really ashamed. I don't know how that guy got in here."

"Oh Gene," he said, "Don't give it another thought. It's a short life and we have to be nice to the phonies too."

His statement amazed me. Duke had known the guy was a fake all along.

If not losing your cool when pressed is a mark of true class, then 'Sir' Duke certainly had no peers in his realm.

Stan Kenton

Those who knew Stan Kenton, a tall, gangly man with a warm, almost Lincolnesque appeal, regarded him as an outspoken, hard-working gentleman who took the ups and downs of the band business in stride. He had a purist's dedication to his music, and was respected in the business as a dedicated and no-nonsense leader. Kenton had strong, if controversial opinions about music, and if provoked did not hesitate to express them. He maintained that jazz didn't always have to "swing," that it could have more harmonic texture and not necessarily be captive to rhythm all the time. His approach to composition and orchestration was decidedly heavy. As a result, his music was serious and dramatic, and immediately recognizable as 'Kentonesque.'

Watching him present his music was stimulating. He often stood at the piano conducting his orchestra with sweeping movements of his long arms, his face a mask of changing expressions—pain, joy, exuberance, encouragement, crescendo, fire—totally involved in the moment.

I especially admired Stan and his band because they produced musical fireworks. Sooner or later, in every arrangement, the music would climax in blazing brass fusillades and dynamic rhythmic intensity. He also consistently showcased an amazing array of exceptional soloists like Maynard Ferguson, Shelly Manne, Art Pepper, Mel Lewis, Shorty Rogers, Kai Winding, Bill Harris, Vido Musso, Lee Konitz, Charlie Mariano and singers Anita O'Day and June Christy.

We played Kenton to a sell-out crowd in Bridgeport at our 'Cocktails and Concert' venue—our biggest crowd to date. The audience loved his unique, screaming big brass sound and the broad reach of the involved, almost Wagnerian-like arrangements. It was a fine show for Kenton fans and a huge crowd turned out. Our net profit from the show was $1,200.

The next night we had rented the Hartford Bushnell Auditorium to present our second Kenton concert (without cocktails of course) in the theater. When driving up the Merritt Parkway to Hartford with Kenton in Bill Goglin's red, four-door Toronado, the conversation got around to the styles of various bands. I mentioned how well Basie and his ever-popular group had done with the crowd when he had played our 'Cocktails and Concert' night.

"He has a great outfit, don't you think, Stan?" I said. "It swings so naturally."

Critics sometimes faulted Kenton for what they regarded as his heavy-handed orchestral approach, which may have inhibited the band's 'swing factor,' though the sound always did generate excitement. He must have been sensitive about it, because when I mentioned Basie, he grimaced slightly, like a contemplating Beethoven, as if he were pained by my comments. He hesitated before answering. Looking out the window at the spring-budding Connecticut countryside whizzing by, he said quietly, but quite sincerely, "You know, Gene, once you get past that incredible, awesome, unbelievable swing, they're really playing Little Bo Peep."

I understood his point completely.

We lost exactly $1,200 on the Hartford concert.

Woody

On a late night flight from Pittsburgh to New York I happened to be sitting across the aisle from Woody Herman. *Free Spirit*, my present band, was then playing a three-week engagement at a large club near Pittsburgh in Greentree, Pennsylvania. I was heading back to Connecticut, aboard the Capitol Airlines red-eye for my day off.

I had produced Woody in concert several times and always found him to be unaffected and extremely approachable. We chatted some small talk. He asked what I was doing with the *Jazz Giants*. Almost ashamed to admit it, I told him the Giants had died of natural causes, but that *Free Spirit* was currently very successful commercially.

"Great, Gene. Glad to hear it. I'm sure it's good. Keep playing."

Woody's bands throughout the years were always of the highest caliber, and his commitment to big band jazz was unmistakable. His bands always had fire, originality, precision and energy. He had the ability to attract the finest players and hone them into an incredibly effective team, understanding them, developing them both personally and musically. Stan Getz, Zoot Sims, Al Cohn, Bill Harris, Ralph Burns, Shorty Rogers, Neal Hefti, Urby and Jack Green, Terry Gibbs, Jake Hanna, Kai Winding, Bob Brookmeyer, Sonny Costanzo, Sal Nistico, Nat Pierce. Nick Brignola, Red Rodney, Frank Rossilino, Richie Kamuca, Carl Fontana and Steve Royal were a few of the jazz greats who played in "Herman Herds."

Woody knew what he wanted, and with extraordinary leadership he always seemed to attain it. He chose excellent musicians, then insisted on their best performances every moment. He wasn't a nitpicker, but he wouldn't stand for sloppiness. He set and maintained high standards, producing some of the most brilliant big jazz bands the world has ever heard.

To me, along with Kenton, Basie and Duke, he was in an exclusive class of men who were superb leaders in the golden age of big-band jazz, and who earned every jazz musician's personal respect, much the same as Dave Brubeck has by those who have been privileged to know him. No one, as far as I know, has ever had a negative word to say about Woody's integrity or musicianship.

On our flight that night I complimented him on the many wonderful big bands he had over the years. One "Herman Herd" always seemed to surpass the previous edition with fresh energy and excitement, and even finer soloists.

"How did you decide on the sound and style for your bands, Woody?" I asked. "Each Herd has had a different sound, yet they're always immediately identifiable as Woody Herman."

He smiled. "I just listen to Ellington and Basie and take what's left," he said.

"Come on, Woody, really, your bands are always powerhouses, always dynamic, always unique, swing like hell.

"No secret. That's what I do."

A few years later year, I heard his band at a Chicago jazz club on my group's night, off during our engagement at the Bonaventure Hotel on North Michigan Avenue. His band was ripping it up, playing brilliant big-band jazz. Bill Chase, the bull-like lead trumpeter, led the charge. Other new, young, super talents had recently joined the band. When we spoke that night, I asked, "Every musician wants to work with you, Woody, how do you always get all these incredibly talented young guys to go out on the road and blow their brains out for you?"

"Gene," he said quietly, and quite sincerely, "What do I know? I'm just a dumb Polack."

It struck me that for one of the greatest jazz bandleaders ever to grace the world's stage, egotism had no voice. His love of music and body of work spoke for him. I could only envy such a state of mind… and such a man.

Brubeck

The musicians I respected most had all been big band leaders, men who had paid their dues and succeeded in bringing the world great big-band jazz. As far as I was concerned, they never lost their self-respect or the respect of others. All were consummate musicians. Each heard the sound of their own concepts and persisted with them through all the vicissitudes of the music business. Each knew the unique challenge and joy of organizing and sustaining a successful big band.

One man I've always respected as much, if not more, is one *not* noted for being a big band leader, although at one time he was. His fame is associated with his work with his unique quartet.

Pianist and composer Dave Brubeck is an extraordinary man, one who never compromised his musical or personal values. He became known across the world performing jazz the way he heard it. During times when most jazz musicians were involved primarily in established duple and triple-meter time signatures, i.e., 4/4, 3/4 and 6/8, Dave's *Time Out* album, which successfully experimented in less common jazz time signatures, was, and is today, one of the largest selling jazz records of all time. Notable among its many hits was "Take Five" in 5/4 time.

Brubeck recorded over one hundred albums and still records and tours at the age of eighty-five at this writing. Juxtaposed with the mainstream of jazz, he is truly an innovator, a genuine, original American music icon.

But there's more to the Brubeck story. Something else sets him apart from others. Not only is he a man of rare integrity, he is a consummate father and family man. He and his multi-talented wife Iola raised six children—five boys and one girl, several of whom are professional musicians in their own right and who have recorded with Dave. The couple managed to keep their family together through all the difficult early years of traveling, moving, insecurities, lack of money, separations and doubt. Not a simple challenge in the entertainment business. Dave never seemed to put his music before family, yet he achieved enormous success and popularity. His was a doubly difficult task, yet he has been hugely successful on both fronts.

Another front affected his life, and in a certain way brought us together. During World War II, Brubeck was a young GI in Europe. German forces had broken through the American lines in a massive, last ditch, counter-offensive at Bastogne, Belgium. Swift moving German Panzer tanks and thousands of troops had pincered the trapped American forces in the famous Battle of the Bulge. For many weeks in frigid cold and snow the battle raged. Losses were heavy on both sides (over 100,000 casualties) making it the largest single American Army battle of the War.

GENE HULL

Dave and his men managed to escape. Eventually the Germans were turned back, which reversed the tide of the war, sealing Hitler's fate a few months later.

Deeply affected, Dave was inspired to write a composition called "Hymn for Conquest," which he arranged with the famous Stan Kenton band in mind. Later Dave approached him with the arrangement.

At that time the Kenton band was recording Pete Rugulo compositions, and Stan was more or less enamored with his work. It was the style he wanted for his band at the time. So Kenton told Dave he wasn't interested. "Sorry, but no thanks," and refused to take the arrangement. The score stayed packed away in Brubeck's footlocker for many years.

Much later I asked Stan about it. He said he didn't recall the incident on the day of the concert Brubeck was an unknown at the time—but after the war Stan was told about it. "I'm sure that was just another one of my more stupid mistakes," he said.

In the spring of 1964 my band, the eighteen-piece *Jazz Giants* was to perform a major concert at the Shakespeare Theatre with the famous Brubeck Quartet – Dave on piano, saxophonist Paul Desmond, drummer Joe Morello and bassist Eugene Wright. Some months before, I read an interview about Dave in which he told of the Kenton incident. I called him and asked if he still had the arrangement. He did. Since our concert together was coming up in a few months, I asked if he'd like us to play it. He said he'd be honored, so we rehearsed the score.

When Dave conducted the piece at our joint concert, he lit up like a kid. As far as I know it was the first time he had heard "Hymn for Conquest" played publicly, almost twenty years after he had written it—a somewhat delayed world premier.

At the time, I worked for a jazz radio station in Connecticut, WJZZ-FM, as sales manager. For a few years Dave was the Advising Music Director. It was labor of love for him. A living for me. In all the times we encountered each other, on stage, at rehearsals, visits to his home in Wilton, Connecticut, at the office, or years later when I visited him backstage after one of his concerts, he never changed—always a graceful, soft-spoken man with humorous sensibilities.

Several years later I hurried into his dressing room after one of his sold out concerts at Tanglewood, in Lenox, Massachusetts. He was standing at the door unassumingly, quietly greeting everyone. I hadn't noticed him as I hurried past into the crowded room. I thought the tall, friendly slim person in the white dinner jacket I saw peripherally was a guard or a friend or someone of no consequence. I never looked up to see who it was. I said hello to Iola, looked about and asked. "Where's Dave?" She smiled and looked past my head.

"Right here, Gene" a voice at the door said, as I turned around. "Just waiting for you to say hello."

Hello Dave, wherever you are. I am proud to have called you friend.

*

Woody, Sarah, Kenton, Basie, Ellington, Brubeck—you told it like it was. Beautiful. See? You don't have to streeeeetch things. Congratulations.

(Thank you. You can trust me from now on.)

Oh, really?

**

Sixteen

"FATHER OF EIGHT OD's"

I held on to the bathroom sink, fighting the blurs. In the mirror I could just about make out the shape of a head. In place of a face was an amorphous mass, a fuzzy, unrecognizable blob. Was moisture obscuring the image? *Swipe the mirror with my hand.* No change. Where was my face? This was like one of those real-life TV police chases where the camera blurs out the face of the captured felon so you can't tell who it is. I opened my eyes as wide as I could; brightness, but no focus. Eyeballs throbbed, assaulted by punishing light.

In a cold sweat, I leaned against the sink and splashed cold water on my face, splattering my shirt, still not able to focus. My head thumped like an automobile tire with a bulge in it.

Pulse weak. Heart racing. Legs rubbery. Hands numbing. How did I get here? What's happening to me? Am I dying? Am I drugged? Never having taken any kind of drugs before, I had no idea what effect an overdose might produce, but this might be it. Desperate not to pass out, swallowing and gulping air as if my lungs were a sieve, I slumped to the floor, fighting to remain awake.

As I sat there, the imagined headlines of my hometown newspaper flashed across my mind: NOTED LOCAL MUSICIAN, FATHER OF EIGHT, OD's IN NEW YORK CITY DRUG DEN. It shocked me into consciousness. What would my family think? How could I let this happen? I should have seen it coming.

By 1972 *Free Spirit*, my six-person showband, was regularly booked at resorts in the Bahamas and Florida during the winter months. The booking dates indicated our success—engagements in the south during the winter months and up north during summers. In the early years of the group it had been just the opposite.

On one of these tours, Steve, our drummer at the time, met a particularly interesting young woman. We were appearing in the Tradewinds Lounge at Nassau's Loews Paradise Island Hotel, a resort that has since been assimilated into part of the present day Atlantis Resort complex.

Diane was a vacationing guest, a striking figure of a woman, about thirty, athletic, dark-haired with a shag cut. A sophisticated NYU graduate, she had a responsible position as Sports Equipment Buyer for Macy's in New York. Everyone liked her. She and Steve hit it off well, laughing at private jokes between themselves, partying at night after the job, and frequently spending afternoons snorkeling together. She was an excellent swimmer, a winsome, alert, 'all-American girl.' At least that was my perception of her. But as I've indicated, at times I could be a bit naive.

A week or so after we had returned from the Nassau engagement, Steve called me at my home in Connecticut. Explaining that he was visiting Diane at her New York apartment, he suggested that the next time I came into "the City" I should stop in, say hello, and have a drink with them on my way home. They'd love to see me. I agreed to meet them the following week.

During those times, between extended traveling engagements, I'd drive into New York City once a week from home for the day, make the rounds of music agents and contacts and have a saxophone or flute lesson with Joe Allard in midtown Manhattan before heading back to Connecticut.

The day I planned to meet them became a full one. I had played a three-hour recording date with Clark Terry, Milt Hinton and Herbie Hancock, had my sax lesson, and later endured a long but necessary meeting with my manager, Dick Towers. I called Steve to say that since it was already eight o'clock and I had a ninety-minute drive back to Stratford, I would have to beg off on coming to visit them. I'd try another time.

He insisted, however. "Aw, come on, boss. We're opening a special bottle of wine just for you. You don't have to stay long. Diane is looking forward to it."

About thirty minutes later I found the upper West Side address on Riverside Drive, an older, but well kept, fifteen-story gray brick apartment building with large windows. It was the kind of building that appears to govern its corner like a big-brother centurion of old New York. I wondered how many thousands of self-absorbed people had inhabited its recesses, walked its halls, painted its apartments, ridden its elevators, screamed, laughed, made love, cried and died there. New York renews itself so often. If only the buildings could tell what they have seen. Tonight would be another moment to store in this one's silent memory bank.

The apartment building crested a higher elevation. It faced the park below, the darkened Hudson River beyond, and in the distance across the river, the nighttime twinkling of the Palisades.

I parked on the street, put my sax case in the trunk and locked the car. The doorman let me into the building and buzzed upstairs to let the occupants of 6-C know their guest had arrived. Very efficient. The elevator hummed up to the sixth floor.

"Welcome, Gene. Come on in." Diane greeted me with a hug and wet kiss on my cheek. "Good to see you again. You're just in time. This is my younger sister, Clare. And Steve is here helping us celebrate my birthday." Extra smiles all around. Their eyes looked particularly mellow and dilated to me. *Hmm.*

"Nice to meet you, Clare. Happy Birthday, Diane. I didn't know it was your special day. I would have brought flowers."

She laughed. With an inviting smile she said, "Oh, it was last month, but it's a good excuse for a party."

For a musician who had been around a bit, my street savvy was not exactly world class—a result of my vanilla up-bringing, most likely. But it didn't take a wizard to figure out this scene. "Steve, can I talk to you a minute?" I said. We walked into the small kitchen. "You guys are obviously partying. And that's fine. But I'm really not into it. Besides, it's late, and I'm tired. Time for me to go home."

"Aw, come on, boss, loosen up. Don't be so uptight. Have a glass of wine and a few nibbles. You're here. Relax for a little while. Don't rush off."

"All right, but only for a few minutes."

I sat on a large upholstered couch, the old soft kind; if you don't sit upright and forward, you sink way back into it. I ate a handful of peanuts, a couple of chunks of cheese, a bite of pastry and sipped about half a glass of red wine. The wine didn't seem like anything special, but it was relaxing. On the walls of the dimmed, high-ceilinged room hung an eclectic mélange of prints and collected artifacts—from Klimt to Wyeth to Warhol to African masks and woodcarvings, to Mexican clay figurines. The stereo produced appropriate soft-jazz musical wallpaper, resonating warmly off the polished hardwood floor.

Diane and Steve sat next to me. Clare, the well-designed tawny-haired sister, sat opposite me on a leather easy chair with her legs folded under her . She exuded the restrained confidence of a sensual woman who has a model's looks and knows it. The three of them were chatting, snacking, laughing. I enjoyed my wine and told them about the recording session that day with some true jazz greats. They seemed impressed. The atmosphere was convivial, and I was beginning to loosen up. *Maybe I'll stay for a half hour.*

Suddenly Diane reached over and snapped open a vial under my nose. It looked like a smelling salts container.

Steve said, "Breathe in, Gene. You'll like it." He and Diane were giggling. Her sister watched without expression.

"What is it?" I said.

"Go ahead," said Steve. "Take a good whiff. Smell it."

I did so. Repeatedly. Big long whiffs. "So? What's the big deal?" Then everything started to whirl around me. What was happening? "I don't feel so good," I muttered, falling back deep into the couch, eyes closing. I tried to get up. Legs and arms leadened. I couldn't move.

"You'll be fine, man," he said, laughing. "It'll wear off in a few minutes."

Clare could see my face. She must have realized I was in trouble, because, as she told me later, I was turning gray. Obviously, I was about to pass out. She stood me up and walked me across the large room to the bathroom. I could hardly move. "Just splash some cold water on your face," she said. "Take your time. Don't worry, you'll be alright."

The other two were now laughing. They had proudly turned on a 'square' to his first and only experience with an *amy* – amyl nitrate – a drug sometimes utilized to revive angina heart patients, a popular toy of sophisticates who were into recreational drugs.

Unfortunately, since it dilates the blood vessels, one of the side effects can be to lower the body's blood pressure dramatically. I didn't know it at the time, but I was already in the throes of blood pressure problems. As a result, the usually mild drug hit me like a sledgehammer. For some strange reason, at that moment I imagined the façade of the building looking at me, frowning, shaking its head like an animated cartoon. I must have been hallucinating.

Red-eyed, confused, weakened and absolutely panicked, I slumped onto the bathroom floor. I don't know how long I stayed there. But I knew I had to get up. I couldn't let myself pass out, couldn't die like this. Maybe out on the street or in my car. But not here. Certainly not here. The headlines were still flashing in my mind. What would my family and friends think? This wasn't my life.

I reached up to the sink with both hands and pulled as hard as I could. *Come on. Push up.* My head bumped into the sink. I hit the floor again. Got to get out of here. An ambulance may come. Or maybe the police. Oh, no.

I tried again. Half standing, resolving not to fall, I looked into the mirror, eyes not seeing clearly yet, my face still a blotch. I forced myself to bump out of the bathroom, wobbling, shirt soaked, feeling blood from a cut on my head trickling down my cheek like the beginning of a tiny warm brook.

"I have to go home. I think I'm dying. What, what did you do to me?"

"Jesus, Gene, you look like shit," Steve said. "It's only supposed to give you a quick little high. It doesn't last long. Don't worry." But the sound of his voice told me he was alarmed. I was too. *Got to get out of here.*

Fortunately, Clare came to the rescue again, supporting me under my shoulders.

"Come on, Gene," she said, "we're going to walk it off." Next, into the elevator, out onto the sidewalk, across the street, down an embankment into Riverside Park. We sat on a bench, while I breathed deeply trying to recover from the panic. Then she walked me back and forth for an hour or so, never letting go of my arm. I noticed the front of the building again, and imagined it was watching the whole scene, keeping score on some invisible tablet, dispassionate, indifferent, but not missing anything. The other buildings would know soon, I was sure.

For a long time I couldn't speak. When I did, I asked her what I had inhaled so freely. She told me it was an *amy* and that I had had an unusual reaction.

"Yeah, I guess." So much for the all-American girl and the smiling drummer. Wait till I get my hands on Steve.

"An *amy*, huh. Some joke." I was too weak to vent my anger. I just wanted to get away from there.

My head cleared gradually as I drove cautiously up the West Side Highway, onto the Hutchison River Parkway and connected to the Merritt Parkway, fifty more miles to Stratford. A roadside cantina black coffee jolted my brain and revived me somewhat. The more my mind cleared, the more outraged I became. How the hell could Steve have done that to me? What kind of a smart stunt did he think he was pulling? What were they thinking? Years later I found out that in extreme cases amyl nitrate can cause death.

I got home at three in the morning, kissed my sleeping children and wife gratefully and slipped into bed feeling lucky to be alive.

"How did it go today?" she mumbled.

"Oh, fine."

*

Scary stuff. You were lucky. Too serious to kid about. I guess I can go back to sleep now.

(Good night.)

**

Seventeen

SOMETIMES I HATED LYRICS

Free Spirit, a premier musical lounge act at a time when many such groups were touring the nation's clubs, hotels and resorts, played mostly pop music, a little jazz, and covered many of the better current MOR (middle-of-the-road) top-forty hits.

One feature that distinguished us from the pack was our excerpt vignettes from Broadway musicals, which we customized into highlights of our shows. Our sound was unique too; we integrated our voices together with our instruments in a way that produced the effect of a much larger ensemble than just six people.

The group was a far cry from the *Jazz Giants'* big-band sounds of former years; and as such, it marked a considerable alteration in my musical direction. Survival had dictated a change of 'religion.' I was weaning myself from the altar of jazz. 'Steady money,' as the musicians called it, had become the necessary goal. One can give for art's sake just so long. As my friend Tiny at the Musicians Club used to say, "Jazz don't pay the rent."

Free Spirit was designed to entertain nightclub audiences with clever arrangements, humor, and solid showmanship by first-rate musicians. Though not a jazz group, it did present a valid variety of music with jazz-flavored arrangements. The fact that we pleased so many people who paid to see us perform, confirmed my belief in the project. There is nothing like paying customers to confirm one's validity as a performer.

Before *Free Spirit*, I hadn't paid much attention to much of the day's pop music, other than the big swing bands when they were also on top of the pop world. In fact, as a semi-snobbish, discerning (I liked to think) musician, I had gradually developed a somewhat fuzzy credo that maintained if a pop song had words, it probably was because the music wasn't good enough to stand on its own. How ridiculous. Of course that didn't include the great standard tunes of the era, but it did embrace most of the shallow tunes of the day.

As if that weren't enough, vocalists had gradually replaced big-bands in popularity, much to my chagrin. Most of the major pop singers were lacking in anything I could call artistic sensitivity. It wasn't just that I resented the success of some of the minimally talented ones who were getting rich singing drivel. I felt let down and insulted, as if my musical training had been a waste. As far as I was concerned, most pop singers weren't even musicians. I cringed every time I heard Eddie Fisher drop a beat. or add an extra one, or sing out of tune. To make matters worse, it was the silly ditty songs that often became the big hits. I was appalled by the declining taste of the mass American market.

Frankly, as far as I was concerned, 50s music was mostly crap, and I never paid much attention to it. The ballads were often insipid: "How Much is that Doggy in the Window?" Bouncy tunes were mostly repetitive nonsense –"Rock Around

The Clock," a case in point. And as for the 'Doo-Wop' style, my prejudice ran so deep that I just about tuned out that whole decade of pop music and its lyrics. To my mind, most of the music of that era appealed to the lowest common denominator of musical taste and set popular music back to a simplistic level. I had spent a lifetime trying to cultivate an appreciation for excellence in music, so I wasn't buying any of it.

In retrospect, I realize that it was just fun—a harmless lightweight distraction that helped many people feel good. But back then music was just too serious to me to see it screwed up like that.

Given the limits of taste I had placed about me to guard against such aural insults, it wasn't until 1964, when my young teenage son David had me listen to a new English group, that I came back to being interested in pop music and contemporary lyrics again. *The Beatles a cappella* arrangement of "Because," in particular, was a work of sheer beauty. As were "Eleanor Rigby" and "Something." Thanks to him I became a fan, not of their antics, but of their music. They pushed out the parameters of popular song, both in content and form.

Broadway musicals weren't high on my list of hits for a time either. In fact, I was down on most songs with words, as I have said. Not the work of great lyricists, like Cole Porter, Jerome Kern, Ira Gershwin, Harold Arlen, and other fine writers, but lyrics in general. In my opinion they were mostly ditties for people who didn't understand jazz, which of course I presumed I did. So that made me a musical authority.

Musical snobbery is second only to intellectual snobbery on the snob chart. I was right up there with the best, or worst, of them. I reasoned that if pop music had no room for improvisation or swing, it was inherently inferior.

Fortunately for me, by the time *Free Spirit* was formed in the 70s, I had outgrown some of my ignorance. The infectious, incredible funk of Motown music stimulated me. And hot horn groups like *Blood Sweat and Tears*, and *Chicago* had a 'cross-over' influence on the pop music scene, and on me as well. At the same time I learned featured songs from *Music Man* and *Fiddler on the Roof*, studied the words, and went to see many Broadway musical theater performances for the first time. You might say it was my time of pop music and Broadway enlightenment.

My narrow perception of what constituted valid musical art began to expand significantly when I discovered that 'Broadway' didn't have to be corny, and could be a rich source of good music. Musical theater could be immediately appreciated by so many more people. I liked that.

One of the highlights of our shows each night was a ten-minute mini-revue of a Broadway highlight. In Meredith Wilson's *Music Man*, I became Professor Harold Hill for a few minutes, delivering his famous *pièce de résistance*, "Trouble in River City." It was a wonderful number. Certainly it challenged me. I was intrigued by the words, the construction of the music and the way it built to a believable climax. It was a musical vehicle for Harold Hill to persuade the Iowa town's folks to counter the "evil influence" of the local pool hall by starting a community marching band. Hill would of course sell them the instruments, after which he planned to skip town.

Once I started performing these kinds of pieces, I loved them, though I often had difficulty remembering the exact lyrics, never, as I have said, having been much of a 'word man.' It wasn't a major problem, however. When I forgot them, I just made them up.

Occasionally, if my memory decided to take a walk (which was more often than not) especially in "Trouble in River City" — it has more words than any other Broadway piece—the others in the band poised themselves with eager anticipation, just waiting to hear what verbal entanglement I would get myself into and how I would extricate myself.

I always made it through the piece, with the aid of some creative manipulation of instant rhyme and an occasional bit of double talk. I figured that what I lacked in accuracy, I could make up for with dramatic ability and performance skills. After all, they were only words; it wasn't as if I made a mistake in the music. Besides, I was the bandleader.

I still didn't experience a personal commitment to the power of lyrics with the same feeling that the music could communicate to me. Though sometimes very strong, words weren't real for me, so they couldn't be as important as the music.

Then one night something tragic happened that changed everything. Quite unexpectedly, the impossible, the unreasonable, the unbelievable plopped itself in my life, as if a wall of steel was suddenly lowered on the road ahead… immoveable, non-negotiable, forcing me to stop short—a trauma I was powerless to change.

Free Spirit was playing a return, month-long engagement in New York at Shepheard's, the swank, very 'in' supper club at Park Avenue's Drake Hotel. People *dressed* to be seen there. The entertainment program featured a contemporary showband alternating its show-sets with a top DJ. The policy was the leading edge of sophisticated club entertainment in those days. One night at 1:00 AM as we were just about to go on for our third show, the last one of the evening, a telephone call came back stage from my wife in Connecticut.

"What's up? " I said, surprised. "You okay? Kids alright?"

"Gene, listen carefully. I have to tell you something," she said quietly. "Your sister's had a coronary."

"What's that?" I said. My wife was a nurse, so I expected a technical explanation.

"A heart attack."

"Oh my God. Is she okay? Is it serious?"

"She didn't make it," she said.

"Didn't make it? You mean she's dying?"

"She's gone."

"Barbara? It can't be. She's never even been sick."

"I'm so sorry," Connie said. She knew my sister was my closest friend.

The third show was just about to start. The club was packed. It was Saturday night. There wasn't much choice but to go on stage. "Ladies and Gentleman, *Free Spirit*." The show began.

The first several numbers I played and sang the music, as always, but this time without hearing any of it. In my mind's eye I kept seeing my sister and me when we were youngsters performing as a professional juvenile ballroom dance team. We swirled across the dance floor in increasingly rapid turns, did spins and lifts and dips and danced many Astaire-Rogers steps—I in my black tails and white tie, Barbara in a white satin gown. She was careful and somewhat timid; I was the one who was always loaded with confidence. And now I could hear her saying to me so clearly, as she sometimes did when I prepared to lift her for an arabesque or spin in one of our routines, "Genie, please don't drop me."

I'd laugh and say, "Don't worry, I won't."

It was happening again on Shepheard's dance floor. Only this time I couldn't protect her.

The moment came for our musical vignette of *Fiddler On the Roof*, in which I, as Tevya, sang and acted "If I Were a Rich Man." I made it through most of the piece, until the last few lines, when Tevya looks up to heaven and says, "Oh God, who made the lion and the lamb..."

I got as far as saying, "Oh, God..." and stopped.

I looked down. Paused. Breathed deeply. Lifted my head. "Oh, God," I said again. I wasn't performing any more. I was talking to God. And I meant it.

The band stopped. The audience was quiet. I remember thinking in that hole of silence, "You rat, how could you do this? How could you snatch away my sister like that, a forty-one year old mother of four young children? It isn't fair." After a long pause, I finished the song and the show, then drove back to Connecticut.

I was angry at God for the first time in my life. Even if we had differences in the past, my belief was never threatened. But this was different. I didn't talk to Him (or Her) for many years after that. As a matter of fact, our relationship hasn't been quite the same since.

At Barbara's funeral three days later, I didn't shed a tear. I was too angry to cry. Her husband and four young teenagers survived her. My mother was heart-broken. It was one of the saddest days of my life.

Four years later, after a concert performance in a summer theater tent near Boston with Sandler and Young, for whom I was conductor, I came to terms with the grief I was carrying around and bawled all night long in my hotel room. For three days the gushing flowed. And then it was over.

Much later I realized that when the tragedy of Barbara's death hit me so hard that night on Shepheard's stage floor, I could well have folded and quit the performance. But somehow, because of the lyrics, I was able to vent my anger and frustration, to speak one-on-one with God, in a way, and get through it. I hadn't ever done that before, probably because there had been no reason to.

I tried to make some sense of what had happened. There didn't seem to be any. Ironically, it was the words of a song that became the vehicle for communication. Through the words I was able show my anger, albeit silently, to the Main Man. Those lyrics helped me recognize and focus feelings, forced me to confront the cruel reality of sudden death and deal with it as well as I could.

I'm now a true appreciator of musical theater. And as for lyrics, I don't hate them anymore, no matter what stories they tell. In fact, I've listened to them carefully ever since and just let the words speak for themselves.

*

Peace.

**

Eighteen

THE BAND PLAYED ON

Think of your fellow man.
Lend him a helping hand.
Put a little love in your heart.
                    Jackie DeShannon, 1969.

"**Gene Hull, you stink!**" snarled the thin, red-faced, middle-aged woman in the black dress, spaghetti straps askew, hair disheveled, "and so does your music!"

There was nothing I could say. It was New Year's Eve. Some people just do not handle celebrations well, I guess.

1972 had been an eventful year. Israeli athletes had been killed by terrorists at the Munich Olympic Games, foreshadowing dire events for decades to come. Nixon had harvested a landside victory, winning his second term, and with it the seeds of Watergate had been sown. The war in Vietnam was still raging.

But happier news had speckled that year also, events of much less significance—only blips on the divine record of the times—but nonetheless of interest to some. For instance, sixteen-year-old Ulrike Meyfarth of West Germany won the Olympic Gold Medal in the Women's High Jump, the youngest female ever to do so. The Stratford, Connecticut *Raybestos Cardinals* won the United States Fast Pitch Men's Softball Championship for the third time. And *Free Spirit* was booked to play a New Years Eve engagement at the downtown Holiday Inn in Bridgeport, Connecticut. I'm sure if you participated in one of these events, you would remember it.

I was the leader and saxophonist of *Free Spirit*. We were by then a national-touring show band, rather well known in Bridgeport in the 70s, and the closest thing to musical celebrity the City had. The six-person group—guitarist, drummer, bassist, trumpet player, a featured female singer, and myself on saxophone—seldom performed in the local area. The rare occasions when we did usually meant good business for the venue operator.

This New Year's Eve event was promoted as "Gene Hull and *Free Spirit*, Home for the Holidays," a dinner dance to bring in the New Year. I looked forward to playing in my hometown for New Year's, since it meant I could spend extra time with family. Granted, Bridgeport was not exactly the garden spot of the world then, still isn't —actor Paul Newman later referred to it as the world's armpit —but the booking was really important to me. For the father of four boys and four girls, being home for the holidays was a special treat.

Many Connecticut people remembered me from the *Jazz Giants*, which had brought us modest local fame and even some national press. As a result, local interest in my musical doings sustained, and the new group quickly developed a strong following.

GENE HULL

The Holiday Inn charged heavily that night for the "Dinner, Dance and Show"—$40 per couple, which was rather steep for Bridgeport in the 70s. In keeping with show business standards of the times *Free Spirit* always dressed in fancy, color-coordinated, custom-made, designer outfits. We presented ourselves in the elegant attire expected of quality performers in those days. That night the band wore black, white, and silver brocaded vests with black satin lapels, white silk 'pirate' shirts and black tuxedo pants. Lenore SanAngelo (now Lenore Mascar) our dark-haired singer, wore a glamorous looking, long white sequined gown. It definitely wasn't the street wear worn by today's performing groups. This was an 'uptown act' with an 'uptown' look that usually played some of the best venues in the country. This particular engagement was different.

The event was sold out. In fact, it was oversold. And that was the problem. The ballroom, where we were set up, had a banquet capacity of seven hundred. But, judging from the crowd, tickets had apparently been sold for nearly a thousand.

Our first set, at 10:00 PM, lasted an hour. By 11:00 P.M. many people still did not have tables. Temporary places had been set up in hallways, foyers and an adjoining cocktail lounge. There still wasn't enough room. Many of those who had been seated weren't getting their dinners on time, or weren't served them hot, if they got them at all. Bizarre as it seems, some people were taking others' tables when they'd get up to dance, even stealing each others' dinners. Part-time waitresses, hired for the night, were quitting on the spot because of the abuse they were getting, which only made the situation worse.

Obviously some people sensed they were getting ripped off, and apparently feeling entitled to get even, justified their conclusion with outrageous behavior. I felt helpless watching the scene from the bandstand.

After the opening set, people I didn't know came up to me and said things like:

"Gene, this is awful."

"Can't you do something?"

"You should know better."

"This is an insult," invected a large woman in a frilly red dress.

"We never would have come here if we had known it would be like this," said another woman.

"You ought to be ashamed of yourself," still another.

Many thought I had handled the promotion and blamed me for the chaos. I tried to explain, but I could tell from their cynical looks that any attempt to set the record straight would do little to calm the seas. I could understand. After all, they had paid out good money to have a special New Year's Eve, and it was turning into a disaster. They were in pain.

Obviously, the hotel manager was a sleaze. He probably thought he could wing it with smooth talk and gloss over temporary inconveniences to customers. But it wasn't working out that way.

When I suggested to him that since people were getting downright hostile he might want to put the overflow crowd into the back lounge at the far end of the hotel and set folks up with a complimentary drink, possibly accompanied with an apology, he told me to mind my own business.

His response didn't exactly thrill me. "Sure, no problem," I said, "if that's the way you want it." But in view of his attitude and the ruse he was trying to pull off, and considering all that was going on in the ballroom, something told me I'd better ask him right then for our money. I hesitated to do so. Even though it was so stipulated in my contract, I knew it would be unpleasant, and I didn't enjoy confrontations.

"I'd like to be paid now," I said, "if you don't mind. It's intermission. And we have to drive to the airport immediately after the job to catch an early morning flight to Florida. It would save time if we took care of business now."

"Are you nuts?" he said. '"Can't you see I'm busy? See me when the night's over."

"Nope. Sorry. Pay us the balance you owe us now in this intermission, like it calls for in our contract, or we pack up and leave... now." (I remembered what happened when I was a kid playing at the White Eagles Hall.) I could see by his expression that he knew I would. He also knew that if that happened, handling the crowd would be even more difficult for him.

We went into his office. He gave me a snarly glare that said, 'You sonnovabitch,' and paid me in cash. Grumbling. Surly. Sour-faced. Swearing. But he paid.

"You'll never work here again," he said. Like I'd want to. I liked him even less.

There wasn't much we could do about the situation except play our music, entertain the best we knew how, and try to help some of the people have a good time. A few minutes before midnight we played the usual "What Are You Doing New Year's Eve," a slow ballad, which our Lenore sang smoothly, expecting people to get warm and cuddly. Couples jammed the dance floor all right, but soon were packed together to a point of immobility. Many couldn't get there and danced next to their tables.

Then came the traditional dramatic countdown: "Ten. Nine. Eight. Seven. Six," etc., "HAP-PY NEW YEAR!" after which we went into a loud, ceremonial rendition of "Auld Lang Syne." Lenore was the only one who knew all the words. I still don't know what they mean. There wasn't much hugging and gentle 'midnight kissing' at the traditional big moment on the dance floor. Couples bumped into each other for more space. Butts smacked into butts. Elbows poked backs. Shoulders jarred off-balance couples that were attempting semi-fancy terpsichorean moves. Heels purposed onto nearby feet, seemingly bent on inflicting un-neighborly discomfort.

Yet through it all, a few inseparably dedicated kissers took it all in stride, clinging, hugging, slurping, standing in place, not missing a single moment of the opportunity for full body contact in a public place. One embracing young couple was jostled to the floor, a tall thin young man and a short, well-built dark-haired miss. They never stopped kissing. From what I could see, the back of the young woman's gold lame' blouse had deserted the area of her black velvet slacks and was heading toward her neck. It wasn't possible to tell if this was a 'wardrobe malfunction' or if the blouse's trip had help from her partner. However, I don't think they were even aware they were in a prone position. Most people were definitely not in such an affectionate mood.

We quickly segued into the usual New Year's Eve ritual of merry nonsense songs like "Pop Goes The Weasel," "Mexican Hat Dance," "Hokey Pokey," etc., to lighten things up. But with all the pushing and shoving that was going on, and the grumbling around us getting louder, we could sense an undercurrent boiling up. Things were about to blow.

We didn't dare stop playing. Instead we began to perform our medley of message songs from the flower-children era of the 60s—the *sine qua non* of every self-contained showband touring the country at the time—with their bright, peppy beat and innocent, if naïve, 'peace and love' message. Vainly we gave it the full evangelical treatment in hopes this would influence the prevailing agitation. The medley was one of our signature numbers, an extended showy-dance piece that built like the "Twelve Days of Christmas" with each of us singing a verse, and the whole group pouncing on the hook-line, "Put a Little Love In Your Heart."

Our intention was that the good vibes we were sending out so sincerely, all the while smiling our winsome best, would soothe the crowd and help them overlook what was, after all, a minor inconvenience compared to the larger picture of World Peace and Brotherhood of Man. It was worth a try, I thought. But my understanding of human-nature-under-stress proved to be somewhat lacking in reality.

Of course, there was a time when certain songs could have a quelling effect on unruly or noisy crowds… like playing the national anthem did back in the era when reverence for the anthem really mattered to people in America. But those days had evidently passed.

Anyway, that was just about when a fight broke out somewhere in the back of the ballroom. There were too many people on the dance floor for us to see what was happening, but we could hear the commotion. In a few minutes, as the shouting got louder and screams more penetrating, we realized this was more than a usual New Year's Eve shoving duel between two drunks.

Stepping up the fervor factor, we fairly bellowed out the song's punch line (no pun intended). "Put a Little Love In Your Heart."

Then…CRRRASSSSH! We heard a banquet table fall. Dishes and glasses shattered to the floor. A rotund, rosy-cheeked woman, bedecked in costume jewelry, screamed as her husband took a wild swing at a tablemate.

Did we honestly think the crowd would kiss and make up? Or get all warm and fuzzy because of our love medley? Talk about naiveté. Still we persisted.

"Come on you people now.
Smile on your brother.
Everybody get together.
Try to love one another right now."

More screams. Punches thrown. Tables collapsing. Women shoving. A football-player-type young man shoved two tussling drunks away from his girlfriend, sprawling them into a falling table. We didn't stop playing or singing. And the crowd didn't stop swinging—fists, handbags, chairs—pulling hair, kicking shins and smashing tables.

Nobody was dancing any longer. Certainly nobody was listening to the music. In the interest of personal safety we moved as far back on the bandstand as we could, where, appreciating the irony of the moment, John Iafrate, our young guitarist, couldn't contain his feelings and was doubled over in a spastic fit of laughter. Yet still he managed to keep on playing. British drummer, Cliff Page, clearly relishing the scene, not wanting to miss any of the Fellini-esque action, stood up behind his drums and continued to play. Unrestrained full belly laughs punctuated his attempts to sing. Jerry Merliani, our trumpet player and I were doing our best to get our horns away from the bumping and pushing. I could swear bassist Gary Fineberg was yelling, "Go man, sock 'em." All the while convulsed with laughter, we continued playing.

As we moved back, Jerry and I managed to take up protective positions in front of Lenore, who never stopped singing, to protect her from any stray attack. It was then that chairs began to fly, and bottles went on the wing.

"That's it, guys," I yelled, "let's get out of here... fast." While we were packing up, the New Year's Eve celebrators continued altercations, oblivious to the world around them. It wasn't a fun fight either. People were mad as hell and apparently intent on destroying the place. A man was hanging onto a low chandelier and kicking at anyone unlucky enough to be pushed near him. More sensible patrons were streaming for the exits—out into the freezing First of January morning.

This wasn't happening as it had several years before, when I had been playing with the Tex Beneke band on a hot summer Saturday night in the Texas boonies. This was Connecticut, supposedly more sophisticated than the Wild West, and in Bridgeport, my hometown, where most of the crowd knew me and *Free Spirit*. I was surprised and deflated. So much for the fleeting glory of over-rated fame.

But it was no time to philosophize. Grabbing our horns we scurried off the platform to secure them in the back room. We disassembled other equipment and our portable Shure sound system and black pearl drum set. Within ten minutes we had loaded everything into the two cars and U-Haul trailer waiting for us outside the back door.

By this time some of the remaining crowd had quieted down. But others were still going at it. The place was now half empty.

Suddenly the manager noticed we were about to leave. "Where the hell are you going?' he demanded.

"Florida," I said, "and quick."

"Listen, Hull, you were contracted to play until two AM! It's only 12:40." It was a weightless protest, as far as I was concerned.

Suddenly, a nearby drunk yelled to another, "Let's see how you like a chair in your face, buddy" as he swung wildly, missing his target crashing it against a wall.

"It's not safe in there," I said, just in case the manager hadn't noticed. "We don't want to get hurt."

"You might if you don't finish playing the dance."

I ignored the implied threat. "There is no dance. It's a brawl. Don't you get it?" At that moment an irate woman in a black dress, who apparently knew he was the manager, approached and blind-sided him with her loaded handbag, a full swing to his head. WHUMP! It staggered him, knocking him back against a table.

"You snake, " she said, her eyes flashing venom. She looked over at me, steadied herself and yelled, "Gene Hull, you stink! *Hic.* And so does your music." With that she turned and kicked over a nearby chair, before swaying back though the crowded ballroom, bouncing off people like a pinball. She was ticked and tanked.

As I tried to help the manager up, he pulled a revolver from his inside jacket pocket, pointed it. He got to his feet he shoved it into my ribs, and ordered, "Get into my office, NOW," He was white with rage. I guess he wanted the money back. There was confusion all around. Nobody noticed.

"Come on, Henry, you nuts or something?' There are hundreds of people around here."

"Get going and keep you hands down."

I did as I was told, a step or two in front of him. The crowd was wilder and noisier. We made our way slowly through the lounge, passed the bar. "Look out, Henry!" I yelled, as I pointed across the room with my left arm. He turned his head for a second. As he did, I tightened my body and with all my strength rammed my right shoulder full into him.

The force caught him in the ribs off balance. He tumbled back, half into a chair. As he did, the gun fired, probably into the ceiling. The crowd panicked, and with terrified screams stampeded for exits and windows.

I ran for the back door, dodging obstacles as I did, jumped into the car—the band already waiting—and drove away. It was a New Year's Eve I'd never forget

Gun? Oh, give me a break!

(I thought it sounded more exciting like that. Besides, I thought you were as asleep. Okay, so here was no gun.)

Tsk, tsk.

With that she turned and kicked over a nearby chair, before swaying back though the crowded ballroom, bouncing off people like a pinball. She was ticked and tanked. There was nothing I could say. She stumbled off; the manager was still smarting from her attack.

I turned and quickly left the building.

We drove to Bradley International Airport in Windsor Locks, sixty patchy-ice miles north on I-95. We arrived around four in the morning, emotionally drained, freezing in ten-degree weather, but relieved to be going to sunny Florida. It wasn't until after we began thawing out with hot chocolates, coffee and donuts in the almost empty airport lounge that we began to relax.

A delighted John Iafrate, our young guitarist, still giddy from the excitement of the night, dramatically toasted a cup of coffee, "All right, all you survivors, it's our turn. HAP-PY NEW YEAR EVERYBODY! I hope they'll all be just like this one!"

**

Nineteen

LAS VEGAS

"Every show band wants to play Vegas," said our exasperated agent.

"Sure they do, Teddy. So do we. So why don't you get us a booking there?"

"It's not that easy. Competition is tough." Teddy Purcell was upbeat when selling to clients. But with the acts he represented, he was usually somber when it came time to field the oft-repeated question thrown at him: "Why aren't we playing Vegas?"

At that moment he'd shake his head slowly, as if about to explain that a dear friend just died, before coming out with one of his stock answers.

We could only hope that someday we'd land a booking at the Mecca of live entertainment.

In the 60s and 70s a Las Vegas booking was the high-watermark, a badge of accomplishment for groups that did not have national recordings. The result usually established them as having the right stuff, and had the power to boost a career almost immediately. Lounge acts, in particular, craved the exposure only a Vegas engagement could offer. I wanted that for *Free Spirit*, too. Being the Type-A that I became as I grew up, always setting goals and focusing exclusively on them, I started gearing up for Las Vegas soon after *Free Spirit* was formed in 1970.

Although we gave it an all-out effort in our five years together, and had our share of successes, *Free Spirit* just didn't seem to have what Vegas wanted. It was an excellent group, but I didn't have the contacts, the 'in,' the 'juice,' the connections to get us there at the time. It was totally frustrating. The five-year effort drained me.

Faced with the realization that *Free Spirit* was at a standstill, and had probably reached its potential, I considered getting out of the music business and developing a new career. But I feared the chances of not succeeding—starting over again at something new at that time in my life.

I decided to give one more try at 'making it' with a different group. Not an easy decision. *Free Spirit* members had shared a dream. Disbanding the group would mean more to us than just a loss of money. We would need to separate and we were close friends. Even so, I felt I just couldn't take us where I thought we should be going, and time was running out. It was over. I had to move on.

I was torn between creating a 'record act' with music that would satisfy the public, as well as my own tastes, and developing a unique performing ensemble that might also have recording potential. The second option seemed preferable because it was safer and could generate revenue more quickly. During the next six months a plan developed based on what I had learned about the business over the years. One more group would be formed. It would be my last.

The envisioned group had to be dynamic, visually appealing, have a distinctive sound, be musically interesting, and commercially viable enough to be recorded for the popular marketplace. Excellent musicianship was a pre-requisite. The goal was to be a Vegas act for main rooms, not lounges.

This criteria distilled into a concept: an all-female string quartet—two violins, viola, and cello—a female singer, four men in the rhythm section composed of bass, drums, keyboards, and guitar, and myself playing saxes and electric flute, ten people in all. The repertoire would be mainstream disco-jazz-pop, music with a recognizable musical and visual 'hook'— its female string players.

The project had to have originality, style, looks, and dance appeal in order to sell records and have successful personal engagements. The group's look and sound should be exclusive enough to get noticed, I reasoned. The rest would follow.

Dreaming it up was one thing; putting it together was quite another. Searching for the right string players, I contacted university and conservatory music departments, posted notices in union halls, placed ads in music publications and followed up on various recommendations. I received hundreds of letters from hopefuls all across the country, and auditioned many candidates. I found that the young women were not flexible musically, that is, their interpretation of pop music was too stiff—they couldn't 'swing—or if they could, they were not attractive enough to be 'show people' in a Vegas ensemble. In the surprisingly long process I eventually settled on four excellent classically trained musicians who were beauties, if a bit reticent about being regarded as such—Karen Lundquist, Ethel Abelson, Mabel Wong and Joan Spergel.

I remember the day I found Joan. She had followed up on an ad and sent a tape and her picture as requested. I came to her residence on New York's Upper West Side one afternoon. As I entered the red brick apartment building walk-up, I heard a full rich sound, like a french horn, careening through the halls. Or perhaps a trombone? It evoked the unmistakable assertion of a strong middle-range brass instrument. As I got closer to her fourth floor apartment, I realized the sound was actually a cello, resonating about the empty halls with colossal presence. I decided to hire her at that moment, before even seeing her.

None of the women had ever played in a pop music group before, and all were intrigued by the idea. They were nice people and serious musicians, willing to put in the rehearsal time necessary to prepare. Of course most of them didn't wear make-up, or shave their legs, or style their hair much. After all, they were classical music devotees. Fashion, unless functional, seemed rather shallow and silly to them. But they were very attractive, and as I have said, wonderful musicians. And that meant possibilities to me.

I had borrowed $10,000 from my bank, with no collateral except my name—pretty risky—to finance the project: uniforms, gowns, equipment, instruments, sound system, orchestrations, rehearsal costs. I commissioned various writers to do original arrangements that would capture the musical potential of the group. It appeared to be progressing well on all fronts, except that it was taking far too long to put together. Six months without steady income was difficult, so I played as many 'casual gigs' as I could find.

Finally we were ready to begin rehearsals, the first time I would actually hear the 'sound.' I loved what the arrangers had done. It excited me. It was distinctive, contemporary, vibrant, sensuous. This could be it. This will indeed make a statement. The group was called *Music Maximus.* But agents referred to it as "Gene's String Thing."

To get us booked and off-and-running, I asked Larry Spellman, the dynamic former Vice President at the William Morris Agency, then head of his own company with Marvin Schnayer and Dick Grass, to see us at a rehearsal. He saw the potential immediately and called Joe Scandori, Vic Damone's manager, to tell him about it. Vic's career was in slow motion at the time and Joe was looking for some new vehicle to help take him with some flourish to the 'main room' stages again.

Handsome, dark-haired fifty-ish Damone was certainly one of the top singers in America. He had a million-seller record when he was still a teenager, which was a rarity in those days. He recorded many best selling albums and possessed one of the most perfect baritone voices ever heard—some say the best.

Subsequently, Vic, who was appearing on Long Island, at the time, drove up to Bridgeport on a cold, March Sunday afternoon to hear us. We dressed the four 'string girls' in long red sheath gowns with spaghetti straps and pearl necklaces. For some reason they were reluctant to shave their legs. It was just an audition to them. It seemed dishonest to them, I guess. But we did get them to wear a little lipstick and makeup. They looked *and sounded* stunning.

Our plan was to stage them grouped around Vic. He'd look dashing in his black tux and opened-collar, white silk shirt. For the audition, Lenore, dressed in a white beaded gown, sang counter parts with Vic on some of his songs. Our rhythm section wore black suits and black shirts without ties. I wore a three-piece white suit.

It worked. Damone was sold. Apparently we had the look, energy, and sound that felt right to him. Three months later we were booked into the Congo Room, the main showroom at the Sahara Hotel in Las Vegas together with Damone and another headliner, Don Rickles.

We opened a few days before July 4, 1976, the year of the bi-centennial, a time when overt patriotism was in fashion. This was a once-in-a-lifetime month to be in Vegas, a city without nuance, which has always been over the top in the flag-waving department.

On the day of opening night, Vic personally brought the four string girls and Lenore to a beauty salon, which catered primarily to theatrical people, where they were given complete makeovers—haircuts, styling, manicures, facials and professional makeup. They were knockouts when they appeared on stage that night. The attention they got from everyone from then on was enough to convince them it was time for a lifestyle change. Glamour did not have to compromise their integrity as people or as classically trained 'serious' musicians.

Opening night was a smash success. The blend with Damone and the group was extraordinary. Newspaper reviews glowed with praise for the new look and sound of the "Gene Hull's Strings" backing Damone. The Strip buzzed with inside talk. Cab drivers pitched it to tourists. Something new had hit Vegas. All agreed that Vic never sounded better. Vic was in demand again. New bookings flowed in.

Wherever we went people seemed to know us. We couldn't pay for a drink or a meal or even our hotel rooms. We felt like stars, smothered in the praise and complements that Vegas gives its celebrities of the moment. We were invited to a cocktail party hosted by Frank Sinatra at Caesar's Palace. I was invited to play a pro-celebrity charity tennis tournament at the Riviera with David Janssen, Hugh O'Brien, Abby Dalton, Juliet Prowse, Rod Laver, Poncho Gonzales and others. John Wayne's wife Pia, was my partner (we lost).

I attended a small birthday party hosted by Ann Margret for her husband, Roger Smith. The group landed an important four-week gig opening Hugh Heffner's posh new hotel in Great Gorge, New Jersey, with Ann Margret, Kenny Rogers and Bill Cosby. We were held over for thirty weeks.

For me it was show business nirvana, an awesome high, confirming in grand style the attainment of a goal. But the most fun was yet to come.

The third week of our engagement at the Sahara my mother Marge, then in her seventies, flew out to Vegas to see us. We talked backstage about the Benny Goodman stage show she had taken me to so many years ago at the Lyric Theatre. Chidingly, I told her I would never forgive her for getting me hooked on a horn that day.

It was a great night for her to see our show—'Las Vegas Hotel Employees Night.' I introduced her to many of the celebrities who were there to perform in a special, after-hours late show. Lounge entertainers, headliners, movie stars musicians, hotel workers, taxi drivers, agents, producers from all over the Strip came for the annual FREE big bash. Backstage was a huge party, packed with stars. Booze was flowing, jokes were rolling, and Lenore and the rest of my group were in thrall, mingling back stage with the stars. Wayne Newton, Neil Diamond, Rich Little, Arlene Dahl, Olivia Newton-John, Don Rickles, Paul Anka, Foster Brooks, Dick Shawn, Jerry Vale, Joey Heatherton, Joey Bishop, Redd Foxx, Johnny Cash, Red Buttons, Robert Goulet, Roy Clark, Andy Williams, and many more. It was overload excitement. All these years trying to get a booking in a Vegas Lounge, and now here we were in a 'main room' on the biggest night of the year. Feelings flooded into me that I cannot describe. Maybe gratefulness comes closest.

Many of the male performers used my backstage dressing room that night. Except for Rip Taylor; he used Lenore's.

"Dahling," he said to her as he came out of her bathroom rearranging his wig, "Thank you so much for letting me come in. It's so crowded in Gene's dressing room, you know." Rip's comedy routine about a gay astronaut, who refused to be launched at lift-off without his crayons, was always a showstopper.

During the show Joey Bishop, of the Sinatra Rat Pack, held the stage for so long, far exceeding his allotted time, that Rickles came out from the wings with a broom, wearing a red apron, and started sweeping up. The audience loved it. Joey got the message. Rickles, despite his acerbic public persona, is a sweet and gentle man. I worked with him several times after that.

GENE HULL

Later in the program, when Vic sang the romantic "And I Love You So," with our lovely string quartet grouped around him, Rickles again came out on the stage, this time with Redd Foxx and Foster Brooks. The three of them pretended to sing backup, complete with overt gestures and body language. The crowd of hotel workers roared with delight.

Vic didn't get it until he turned around and saw Don and the other two on stage in back of him. Discovered, Rickles ran up to the mike, knelt down on one knee with feigned sincerity, and began kissing Vic's pant leg, pleading, "Please don't tell Frank."

After conducting Vic's show, I went back to my dressing room and walked in on Dick Shawn "talking" to a young cocktail waitress on the couch. Both were in a diminished state of dress. I turned around and left immediately. I hate interrupting important conversations.

Where else but in Vegas could this happen? My name as musical director was 'in lights' on the Marquee outside on the Strip (my mother took a picture of it) and my group was appearing on the main room stage. The night was memorable, a once-in-a-lifer. In fact, our whole Sahara engagement was an unqualified success. Each show earned standing ovations. I conducted the Sahara's regular eighteen-musician house band, augmented by our string group. Vic seemed totally comfortable and never sounded better. The "Lady Strings", as the local press referred to them, were "a treat for eye and ear," as were Vic's duets with Lenore. The show earned great reviews.

The only exception apparently was Vic's beautiful, young, wife, Becky, a lovely person, who honestly didn't think Vic needed Lenore and the girls around him on stage. I figured the package was so successful that Vic would overlook the fact that she wasn't too keen on it—a business decision, of course.

The package, indeed, was on the mark. Vic was immediately rebooked at a later date to co-star with Lena Horne, who was a delight to work with. What a lovely woman with a perfect, smooth complexion. A consummate perfectionist, she didn't walk through rehearsals; she sang each note full out, rehearsing each musical nuance, every stage movement, every gesture.

Not too many years before, when Vegas was a segregated town, Lena was forced to use the servant's entrance of the Riviera hotel where she was performing but was not permitted to stay. She had to use the kitchen entrance. It was on a return engagement, then staying in the hotel with her family, that her two children used the Riviera's swimming pool one hot summer afternoon. A hotel guest demanded that management drain and refill the pool before the guest's (white) family went in the pool. Management complied. I can only imagine how Lena must have felt.

Damone's career was on a roll again. And as far as I was concerned, a milestone had been reached—Las Vegas. It hadn't come easily, but it was worth the effort. It seemed we had finally put together the right thing at the right time. A mountain had been climbed. I started making plans for all the money I would earn. We all did. The gamble had paid off. The 'business' being what it is, however, something told me not to get too comfortable. Things looked too good.

*

Sounds like you finally made it. But do I sense clouds approaching?

(You ought to know.)

**

GENE HULL

Twenty

MEETING ELVIS

Don't go to Rochester, New York in the wintertime unless you really enjoy winter. Cold, cold, brutal cold. Snow pounces on the place in piles, driven by frigid winds swooping off the Great Lakes. Okay, so it's not as bad as Buffalo. But still it makes you grimace and scrunch up in your coat, scarf, boots and long underwear, wishing you were in Florida.

However in summertime it's a beautiful scene, a place of fresh air, flowers, friendly sunshine, warm days, cooler nights, and relaxed citizens who share the esprit of getting through another winter.

The tour with Vic Damone took us to Rochester, NY, during the summer of 1976, performing for a week at the Town and Country Casino Theater. I couldn't help but appreciate the verdant swath of the whole area, especially after having spent several weeks in Las Vegas surrounded by its scrubby deserts, rock-and-dirt mountains and baked, dry July heat.

Rochester was easy on the eyes, especially for those of us who missed the greenery of the Northeast. After Vegas, I quickly found it easy to relax in this winsome environment, especially after our Vegas gig had been so highly charged.

We arrived at the theater in late afternoon and had a brief rehearsal—mainly to adjust the sound system to Vic's tastes. Each of our string players was amplified with a contact microphone attached to her instrument. As a result, sound balancing took a little longer; but when properly adjusted, the system allowed the string quartet to sound like a full string section—one of the keys to the musical success of the group. Vic left this part of the sound check up to me and usually concentrated on getting just the right attenuation from his mike. He had amazingly sensitive hearing and excellent vocal intonation. He knew just what he wanted to hear, or more precisely what he didn't want to hear.

We opened that night and were well received, even though the sound could have been improved if we had spent more time balancing it. But no matter, we'd "correct it tomorrow."

The next morning we returned to the theater, rehearsed and tweaked Vic's mike. I've never met anyone, before or since, more particular than Vic when it came to the sound of his microphone. Once, after the first night of our initial engagement at Dom Bruno's Club at Sylvan Beach near Syracuse, he and I worked until four in the morning testing and adjusting his mike and the sound system until he was satisfied it was the best we could produce. This happened often on subsequent engagements. The process always took longer than expected and Rochester was no exception. By the time we got back to the downtown Hilton Hotel from the second day's sound check, it was already two in the afternoon.

I had promised the group that the Friday payroll would be ready for them by noon. I rushed up to my room and began counting and recounting the cash for our ten-person group. I was just about to place it into various envelopes, when the hotel's fire alarm started blaring non-stop just outside my door.

Most anyone, including me, who stays in hotels frequently has been through false alarms in their travels. So after opening my door and checking for smoke or any sign of a disturbance – there was none—I decided to ignore the interruption.

After about twenty minutes of incessant, high-pitched clanging, I called the front desk.

"Sir, don't you hear the alarm?" someone said. "Everyone has been evacuated from the hotel. You have to get out. You have to get out now!"

I had several thousand dollars spread out on the bed in counted stacks, and I didn't want to jump up and leave. "What's the problem?" I asked, as calmly as I could.

"There's been a bomb threat. Everyone's left the hotel. You must get out now. And you have to use the stairs." I imagine that a bomb threat in a Rochester hotel in 1976 was a rarity. I mean this wasn't like kids calling in false alarms at school these days to miss a class or a test. The desk clerk was panicky.

"Do you know what time the bomb threat is supposed to be?" I said.

"Three o'clock!" he yelled.

I looked at my watched. It was five minutes before three. Stuffing the cash into my pockets, I ran down seventeen flights to the lobby, past the glass doors, and outside to join hundreds of guests and onlookers on the grass. My watch read 3:05 PM. Fire trucks and police were everywhere. Search teams were in the hotel searching for 'the bomb.'

After two hours the incident was declared a hoax.

Elvis was performing a show at the local arena that night and was scheduled to be staying in the hotel. Apparently, someone assumed that if an afternoon bomb threat were called in, everyone would have to evacuate the hotel—and they would get to see ELVIS. The police caught the pranksters when a few teenagers in the crowd started yelling "We want Elvis." But Elvis hadn't checked in yet. So their scheme had failed. Payday was a little late that Friday.

Elvis finally did arrive at the hotel, via the underground service entrance in back. He hosted an early evening private cocktail reception in his suite prior to his performance that night. Damone knew him and was invited, so some of us went with him to the party to meet The King.

Elvis was already dressed in his cape and white 'suit of light' when we arrived. His svengali-like manager, Colonel Tom Parker, stood a little aside, watching Elvis closely.

I must admit at being somewhat in awe at the prospect of meeting Elvis, even though I had not been a fan of his. Then suddenly, the man himself approached, one of the most famous celebrities ever.

But wait a minute. This was not the vibrant young Elvis I had seen in the movies or watched on television—the slim-hipped, slow talking, fast moving, karate chopping, dashing lad who drove millions of women crazy and made lasting fans of men all over the world. This Elvis was obviously overweight, bloated and puffy faced. Dark circles hollowed his eyes, and he looked completely fatigued. He also seemed to be stuffed into his costume. A massive, three hundred pound, six-foot six-ish bodyguard—probably named Bubba or Tiny—never left his side, and appeared to be in charge of guiding him around the room and meeting people.

When Elvis got to Vic, he and Vic hugged warmly. Introductions followed.

"Elvis, this is my conductor and music director, Gene Hull."

With a warm handshake, Elvis said, "Pleased to meet you, Gene. Vic has told me a lot about you. Sounds great. How 'bout you being my conductor when my man takes a break in a couple of months? Vic'll give you some time off, won't you Vic?"

GENE HULL

"Anything for you, Elvis, " said Vic.
"Are you guys serious?" I said.
"For sure," said Elvis.
"Deal," I said. We shook on it. Too bad Elvis died before I could become his music director.

*

It's a good thing I'm listening. Conductor for Elvis, eh?

(Okay. So it was just a little improvement in the story.
　　　The introduction to Elvis really went like this.)

"Elvis, this is my conductor and music director, Gene Hull." With a warm handshake, a tired Elvis smiled and drew a deep breath, trying to sound upbeat. He looked at me and said in his unmistakable deep, monotone, slurred mumble-jumble something like:
"HeyhiyaGeneyoutheguywiththestringshowyoudoin' everythingalrightbuddy?"
Wide-eyed, dumb struck, *what's he saying?* I wanted to say, "What the hell happened to you, man? You look terrible." Instead I said, "Pleased to meet you, Elvis." We made small talk and he asked how I like working with his "goomba," Vic.
Later when people asked me what Elvis said when we met, I could only say I really couldn't be sure. But it didn't matter. The meeting was a moment I would never forget.

When Elvis Presley died the following year at age 42, weighing 230 pounds, the cause of death was officially announced as a heart attack. It was known that he suffered from anxiety and exhaustion. However, subsequent investigations revealed that he abused various stimulant uppers and depressant downers, prescribed by two different physicians independent of each other. One doctor admitted to prescribing 5,300 tablets for him in the seven months before he died.

Years later I learned that Colonel Parker was really Andreas van Huijk, formerly of Holland, a man who had never been a legal resident of the U.S., and certainly was no colonel. However, he was a colossal promoter, who had successfully propelled and guided Elvis's phenomenal career. In my opinion, he was also at least partly responsible for his gifted client's tragic death.

I've often thought perhaps someone close to Elvis should have 'managed' him more carefully.

**

Twenty One

IT'S GREAT BUT...

One dawn, when the day still belonged to the cool night, I was hurrying through the long, deserted blocks just north of Chicago's Loop on my way to see Vic Damone. The night before, at the conclusion of our week-long appearance at Field's Club in Cicero, he had asked me to come to his hotel suite the following morning for a meeting—an unusual time for us to talk; it sounded urgent. He explained he needed to catch an early flight to L.A.

Several months had passed since the successful Las Vegas debut of our string group with Vic. Our tour took us across the country. Things were going well. I wanted to believe that my earlier concern for the group's success was fueled by the ever-present instability of the music business. I hated the insecurity and wanted to believe things were perfect at last. Unfortunately, insecurity often drives creativity, the fun part.

Hearing my footsteps echo in the empty streets, surrounded by towers of concrete, steel and glass, I began to doubt myself. Much the same as a comic might who gets the blues in advance, fearing the day when the laughter stops. Strangely, I couldn't shake the negative feeling.

Was it the atmosphere? Was it intuition? Whatever it was, I sensed Doctor Doom somewhere ahead, just out of sight. Over the years I learned to pay attention to gut feelings. I stepped up the pace and watched carefully.

Reaching Damone's hotel without incident was a relief—a welcome haven at the end of an uneasy trek. The surroundings were impressive. The first thing I noticed in the deserted lobby was a beautiful arrangement of tall, fresh-cut tropical flowers atop an antique table. Several oversized leather chairs commanded the sides of the area, as if they were regal retreats for important bodies.

How luxurious. How tastefully done. This is what you can afford when you're a star like Damone. Must be nice. I smiled hello at the desk clerk as I walked past to the elevator. He acknowledged with a perfunctory nod. The quiet purr of the well-maintained lift soothed the ascent to the fifteenth floor. The elevator, with its softly lighted panels of dark red oak and brocaded fabric, must have been a quiet cubicle of comfort for hotel guests engaged in necessary up-and-downing. Again, I was impressed.

For a few moments I forgot why I was there. *I'll never be able to afford to stay in a place like this.*

"Good morning, Gene. Thanks for coming. Come on in, sit down, have some coffee."

I poured a cup from the sterling carafe and added sugar.

"Thanks, Vic. "What's up?"

"I want you to know how much I've enjoyed the strings, Gene. Everybody loves them. Lenore and the girls are sweet and talented. And you've handled things very well. I couldn't be more pleased."

GENE HULL

"Well, thanks, Vic. We love you, too. I'm glad the whole package is a success." I smiled broadly, like we were two champions sharing a moment.

"Yes, it's an excellent concept. Looks great, sounds great. But to get right to the point, I want you to be my musical director full time. I mean, without the girls and the group."

"Huh? I thought you just said you really liked the concept."

"I do," he said. "It's great, but... well, my financial advisor," (referring to his third father-in-law, whose daughter Becky was not the biggest fan of our group backing Vic) "advises that the package is just too expensive. I'll have to work without a traveling group from now on and contract local musicians wherever I'm booked. But I'd like you to be my music director-conductor-contractor and travel with me. I'll start you at $750 a week and all expenses."

BOOM! The honeymoon was over. Accepting his offer would mean the end of the string group. Nine good people would be out of work. I reflected on the years it had taken to get this far and the effort in developing a successful group like *Music Maximus.* I thought about the financial investment and about starting over again. I recalled the failures and the phoenix-like successes of some of my other bands. Mostly, I thought about the toll that time exacted.

I wanted to tell Vic to forget it. I wanted to blame him and tell him to take a flying leap. Instead I sipped my coffee. He was only doing what he felt was right for him. And I was feeling sorry for myself.

I told him I needed to think about it and would let him know the next day. True, $750 a week was good money to me in the mid 1970s. But my gut ached when I left the hotel room, knowing I had to make a decision I didn't want to make.

Would I be selling out if I accepted his offer? Would I be letting down the others in the group who believed in me and depended on me and had worked so hard? Yes, of course. I couldn't deny it. But truthfully, I was running out of gas. Leading and managing a ten-piece act on the road, trying to find bookings when we weren't playing with Vic, was more than I could deal with any longer. The years had piled up faster than I could shovel.

During the next several hours, weighing pros and cons that night, the answer consistently came up the same. It would be best to get off the moving train before it stopped. I decided to disband *Music Maximus*, give up the long-shot dream of recording and headlining in Vegas and 'lay up' (as golfers say), play it safe, and become Damone's musical director exclusively. The security the job seemed to offer simply outweighed the unknowns of starting over again.

A few months later *Music Maximus* was dissolved. I explained my reasons to the group and reminded them of my financial responsibilities. Without hitching our wagon to Damone, the future would be too uncertain. There wasn't much choice. A few were really disappointed. Most shrugged it off and said, "That's the business." They were gritty young people who were realistic about the life. But I felt bad for them... and me.

For the first time since I was a kid, I was no longer a bandleader. I was lucky, however. Conducting for Vic proved to be good for me. I had the skills and was good at it. It was what I needed at the time. I toured as musical director with Damone, Sandler and Young, and other celebrity acts for almost three years throughout the United States, Canada and Europe, as well as playing many of the most popular network variety television programs and talk shows.

There were fewer daily responsibilities with this job. I didn't have to worry about bookings, transportation, maintaining a payroll, managing personnel, procuring arrangements, uniforms, equipment, and being the boss. It was

GENE HULL

easy. I just had to make sure the new orchestras in whatever cities we were booked were rehearsed by me and properly prepared to play the celebrity's shows.

Merely conducting, without the responsibilities I had been used to for so long, was fun and actually kind of a heady experience. I got to concentrate on the music. Working with these artists was a privilege, and I met many fine people. Certainly it was an invaluable life course in dealing with extreme personalities. But the cost was great. My marriage had failed. Or more precisely, I had failed my marriage. Too many separations. Too long away from home. Too much time spent losing touch, trying to catch the brass ring. Divorce would follow a few years later. Music, which had given me so much reason for being, seemed to have demanded a commensurate payback.

Finally, I had enough of conducting for celebrities. Steady work was always at the whim of the "stars." Often they took time off, sometimes several weeks at a time. The conductor was expected to fend for himself. There was no real security. Of course, if security were my primary concern I should have gotten a job at the Post Office. But the 'road' was still the 'road'—a circle that eventually returns to where you start. You couldn't build a future on it, especially in my situation with a family to support.

A Peggy Lee song came to mind, "Is That All There Is?" And I thought, as Cy Coleman wrote for *Sweet Charity*, "There's Gotta Be Something Better Than This."

Conducting for an established touring organization that worked steadily, rather than for a single artist, seemed to be the answer. At that time the Ice Capades was the most established and successful touring ice show, booked a solid forty-five weeks a year, featuring high-quality live music, and enjoying a prestigious reputation. They carried a conductor and a nucleus of fine musicians. I had heard that the conductor's salary was well over a thousand a week, and that the work was steady. It seemed logical to target Ice Capades for a job. Again I took aim at a new goal, this time little realizing that I would be starting down a path that would lead to something quite different from what I had anticipated... the exit from a career as a professional musician. The time-to-change clock had ticked again.

*

I see you're getting honest again. And the plot is thickening.

(Of course I'm honest. And yes, it is.)

Hmm.

**

GENE HULL

Twenty Two

SEGUE

Where: New York City

Place: The Waldorf Hotel
           John Kluge's ten-room penthouse suite
Time: Spring, late 1970

Purpose: Meeting with Eric Rill

For several years I had known Eric Rill personally and professionally, and regarded him as a special friend. Eric was a high achiever—*wunderkind* comes to mind—having become president of Ramada Inns of Canada at twenty-eight. Two years later he was appointed corporate President of Ramada Inns Worldwide group, with *more than* 600 hotels in all. (Eric left the business world several years ago and since has authored two successful foreign intrigue novels.)

Eric knew my work with both *Free Spirit* and *Music Maximus*. He was also a friend of John Kluge, one of the world's richest men, among whose many business enterprises was ownership of the Ice Capades. Since I had targeted Ice Capades as a possible job opportunity, I called Eric at his Phoenix office to ask a favor.

"Would it be possible to suggest to Kluge that I might be a good conductor for the Ice Capades?"

Coincidentally, Eric was planning to be in New York the following week and would be staying at Kluge's Waldorf suite. He suggested we meet there, so we could discuss the situation before Kluge returned to town.

When I arrived he showed me around the huge suite—actually, suites—replete with ten elegant bedrooms and baths, a huge main living room with at least four elegant couches, tapestried full-length windows, and a mahogany dining room table which could easily seat twenty-four. He didn't have to point out the original art tastefully situated and lighted on various walls, Renoir's, Picasso's, Monet's and others. A Rodin and a pedestaled, unpretentious Henry Moore sculpture were in evidence. It was a different world.

After my gaping jaw had returned to normal, we sat down to talk. Eric questioned why I wanted to be the conductor for the Ice Capades. "Aren't you tired of traveling, being on the road all the time?"

"I'm a musician, Eric. I have to make a living wherever I can. It's the nature of the business."

"That's not all you are," he said. "I know you. You manage people well. You're honest, and you take care of business."

"I'm glad you think so. But conducting for the Ice Capades would be a steady, good-paying gig, and I could use one right now."

"How would you feel about relocating to Phoenix and working for me at Ramada Corporate? There's an opening coming up. Key Howard is leaving the company."

GENE HULL

"Are you kidding?" I said. "He's the Entertainment Director. He's legend. Make me an offer." He did, and I accepted a position in Phoenix at Ramada's Headquarters.

Entering the corporate world seemed like a solid move. The timing was right. For the first time in non-performing employment, I didn't regard myself as a musician working a day job while looking for the next music gig. I immersed myself totally in the business environment and learned as much and as fast as I could. It was up to me to screen agents from Maine to California, contract bands and plan entertainment schedules a year in advance for each of the sixty-odd hotels that featured live music. DJs worked the lounges of another sixty hotels. I took to the challenge immediately and loved the job, which required that I visit each of the five national zones at least once during the first year. The traveling covered almost every state.

My work was organized, effective, and seemed successful. However, the following year I was caught up in a corporate "re-alignment" when Rill left the company. The new president brought in his own key people. With the inevitable sweep that occurred, my hope for a solid career in the hotel industry vanished as quickly it had appeared.

Once again it was shuffle time. I moved to Las Vegas to start over. I formed Century Artists Corporation, a small partnership with Dick Towers, former manager of *Free Spirit*, booking and producing shows and acts for Nevada hotels. I liked producing but hated booking acts. It was sales, sales, sales—not my strongest interest. But it paid the rent, a living, at best.

This was a difficult time, the period in which I hit bottom. My personal life was in shambles. My career had hit a new low, and the future seemed invisible. At forty-eight I was almost broke. Depression clouded every day. I had little money and an income that went for bills and child support. I lived in a town that didn't care for 'losers'—though it did its best to create them.

234

And since my name was no longer on a Strip marquee, I qualified for non-entity status.

Anonymity is the last thing an ex-performer wants. But I figured it was meant to be. Maybe I deserved it. It was a dark period with much soul-searching for something meaningful to do with my life.

Though this was difficult to gather at the time, it was a good thing. It marked the beginning of a personal rebuilding process that changed my life. No other alternative was acceptable.

The early dream of a music career faded, Although I had attained some notable successes, it wasn't ever quite enough for long enough, and became less and less important. A worthwhile, less ephemeral future, and reuniting with my family became the priorities.

I was now much closer now to accepting the moment many journeyman performers eventually face: separation from performing. At first, letting go is painful. Unrealized dreams of could-have-been tease you. But the truth is, I never considered myself a greatly gifted musician. I had certain abilities, true. But I had worked with many whose natural talents far exceeded my own. My ability to lead, however, and hopefully to inspire people, far surpassed my talents as a player. I was a better-than-average player. That's about it. And I did not think that was not enough.

I realized that because of persistent effort, coupled with the driving passion to succeed, I had achieved a great deal, maybe more than my talent justified. I was grateful for that. But as a young Jamaican woman once wisely pointed out to me in Ocho Rios one night after I had won a bottle of rum at a beach party barefoot dance contest and was gasping for breath, "You can dance, Mon, but you ain't gettin' any younger."

She was right, of course. The clock was ticking. I was ready to find a place in life that did not include having to prove my worth playing a horn. Besides, the Ramada experience had given me a taste of a life on the other side of performing, in which I felt I could make a contribution.

After two years, an opportunity arose that reached up like a silver stairway. A new company in the expanding cruise industry in Florida was looking for an "entertainment person" with "corporate experience" and "Las Vegas expertise" to establish and head its entertainment program. Because of my Ramada position, my time in Las Vegas, both on and off stage, and years of professional experience in various facets of the entertainment industry, I got the job. I was ready to begin a new life... career number two.

Miami, the largest cruise ship port in the world, was my new base of operations. Not knowing anyone there meant it was truly a new beginning for me. I arrived shortly after the 1980 Marielito immigration from Cuba. Tens of thousands of Cubans—mostly good people bitterly opposed to Castro—were suddenly allowed to emigrate overnight to the United States—125,000 in all. They left from the port of Mariel, Cuba, evacuated in a massive American boatlift to Key West. But Castro had emptied the prisons and freed the worst criminals, saying that unless they were included with the massive Cuban exodus to the United States, there would be no boatlift. It was an all-or-nothing situation.

Miami was like a frontier town then. Thousands of displaced Latinos poured in. Money and opportunity, coupled with high crime and cultural clashes, splashed across south Florida. It was the time of the great 80s drug infiltration into the popular culture, and with it the associated violent crime.

Miami Vice was a hit TV show. Cocaine was king and had many slaves. At the same time the city undertook massive redevelopment and high-rise building construction. Business opportunities were unlimited and the economy was booming . It became known as the "Magic City" with both a nightlife and skyline of dazzling color. Latino music resounded in all corners of the town. Latin foods and a vibrant new pulse attracted the world's fun-seekers to Coconut Grove and later to South Beach. Wealth and poverty existed side-by-side, as inseparable as city streets from sidewalks.

Just because it was on the menu didn't mean you had to order it. I could observe the mood without participating. So it was an exciting place to be. A city was being born again, just as I was. I immersed myself in this vibrant new world, resolving that whatever it took, I would make the most of an extraordinary opportunity in the burgeoning cruise industry.

My work as Corporate Entertainment Director of Scandinavian World Cruises involved extensive international travel, especially to Denmark, Norway, Germany, England, France, Greece and Sweden—planning entertainment programs, producing shows, overseeing construction of shipboard showroom refurbishments and new-builds, hiring acts, and establishing the company's shipboard cruise activities programs. Achievements of the past didn't matter to me, and I never looked back.

I was fortunate to enter an exploding new industry at the opportune time. After three years I became Director of Hotel and Casino Operations for Scandinavian World Cruises. Along with this professional growth, I also reconnected frayed ties with my family, the most important undertaking.

Horn playing dimmed to the distant past. Then one night, as I was traveling on one of our ships, the band's trumpet player took ill just before show time. His part was critical to the show, apparently, so a minor panic ensued. When I heard about it, I asked if the tenor sax player had a soprano sax. I borrowed his horn, sat in, and sight-read the show's trumpet parts on soprano. No big deal, considering my experience. But the musicians were surprised. They had no idea that the Entertainment Director was also a musician. From that night on I never had any problem managing ships' musicians.

In 1989 I was recruited by one the world's largest cruise line companies, Royal Caribbean International, where for many years I was the producer of its award-winning production shows and ice shows—the work I loved best. I had the opportunity to work with many exciting young talents—dancers, singers, ice skating stars and production staff, who were far more advanced in their professions than I had been at their age.

It was always stimulating, never boring. There were surprises, like working with Katerina Witt and the likes of Peggy Fleming. The ice shows' fine co-producer, Willy Bietak, a particular joy to work with—creative, organized, honest and affable—is certainly one of world's most important ice production producers today. His staff was well trained and effective; as a result I was able to concentrate on more creative production elements.

There were outstanding young stage and ice production writers, directors, and chorographers—with imaginative minds, dedicated to their craft—Lenore SanAngelo who developed into a first rate writer/director, Mark Dow, Harrison McEldowney, Sarah Kawahara, Willie Bietak, Vickie Davis, Kathy Steele, Sherie Zunker; brilliant scenic designers Brad Kain, Jerry Hariton, Vickie Hariton, and Bob Rang; exciting costume designers Pete Menefee, Jordan Ross and Edwin Piekny; creative lighting designers Peter Moore, Mike Pitzer, and video graphics entrepreneur John Potts—all of them exceptionally gifted— solid support managers Robin Cahill, Jeff White, Sylvia Froescher, and MaryAnn Delany. Brenda Bontiere and her dedicated team produced thousands of production costumes, often dealing with stressful deadlines and extruded budgets, yet always managing to spread kindness and good will to everyone. I learned from all.

Peter Compton, Royal Caribbean's Vice President of Entertainment, and I were recruited at the same time. While his mission was more corporate and involved more planning, mine was more hands on. He was a practical visionary. I was a can-do guy. A symbiotic relationship developed between us that proved extremely beneficial to all. The entertainment product of this cruise line set a standard that became the envy of the industry and remains unequaled today.

A new world had opened up. And because of the experience gained in the crazy up-and-down years as a musician and producer, I was well prepared for it. Frankly, after the insecurities of a long jazz and pop music career, I often felt giddy receiving a corporate payroll check every two weeks. It always seemed like a gift.

Later, life let me unwrap yet another wonderful present. Much to my good fortune, and incredible luck, I met Beverly Myers and was blessed with a strong second marriage. I never imagined such a relationship would happen to me again.

From notes to boats the transition was complete. Seeing life now from a different perspective, I began to mellow. I had found the ideal combination of financial security and artistic creativity. The work and the environment was a seedbed for gaining fresh insights, new appreciations, new interests and new challenges.

New ships were being built in Finland, Germany and France. Refurbishments were sometimes done in Portugal. Many visits to the shipyards were necessary. I brought out each new ship, fifteen in all, from the European yards as they repositioned to their new market places in America, the Mediterranean and the Pacific. In this new life I had the time and desire to smell the roses—not the least of which was appreciating some of the world's wondrous ocean vistas.

I often think that if it weren't for sensitivities gained as a musician, I wouldn't have appreciated this new life so intensely. The sea became an extension of music. I listened to it carefully.

Your conscience is clear, and so is the coast. Proceed.

Twenty Three

VOYAGE

For some the fascination of the sea is a fact of life, mesmerizing, like staring into a campfire or watching a gentle snowfall. It has its own special call. However, this was not so with me.

During ocean crossings for RCCL my responsibility was to ready the entertainment programs on new ships. When a ship was introduced into passenger service, the entertainment venues, shows and systems were expected to be fully operational. In a sense, then, the ocean existed *outside* the ship for me, more of an incidental aspect of the journey. I hardly noticed the sea. My focus and concentration was on preparations and rehearsals. Every moment counted.

By the time of my final voyage as producer for RCCL, I had become more aware of the sea. The shows and entertainment systems were ahead of schedule. Brad Kain, my talented successor-to-be, who is also a fine scenic designer, was on board and had the project well organized. I was relaxed and kept extensive notes, having the time and inclination to observe more of nature's wonders. This was my twenty-fifth crossing in almost as many years in the cruise industry, the last crossing for me, and it began in Turku, Finland.

I arrived in Finland two weeks before the voyage. Unseasonably frigid winter weather for early November, with temperatures dropping to four degrees Fahrenheit, was enough to chill even the Finns. Packed snow and ice covered the ground. Wind was biting. Skies were overcast. But I felt fortunate: the airlines had NOT lost my luggage on the 23-hour flight to Turku. So in spite of the weather, the trip already seemed successful and bound to be filled with good fortune.

As the ship sailed from Masa Yards early on a November morning—with its crew of 1,200, plus construction contractors, a few guests, and RCCL supervisors like myself—billowing clouds of new snow swirled at us from all directions. It was a beautiful, dense snow, though I'm sure the captain didn't care for it. The reduced visibility meant the ship had to inch its way for hours through the early stages of the Finnish archipelago.

Thousands of islands, seemingly broken off from the mainland, as archipelago systems appear to be, scatter for miles into the Baltic Sea. Negotiating a huge ship through the narrow, winding passages at five knots, can be challenging. In the meantime, theater and ice show rehearsals were already under way. The performers welcomed the easy ride.

I wondered how the ocean crossing would be this time. The Navigator of the Seas was the world's largest passenger ship to date, fifteen decks high, a thousand feet long, 144,000 tons displacement, over three times the size of the Titanic, a floating city. Yet. if the seas became unusually rough, we could seem as tiny as a bug on a beach. The massive ocean is unpredictable, rarely calm for very long, sometimes angry and always powerful. I was curious to see how our new ship handled it.

Two days later the ship stopped in Kristiansand, Norway, at the Atlantic end of the Baltic Sea, to disembark travel agent guests before the crossing. Kristainsand is a refueling place for Baltic ocean-going cargo ships and tankers, a quaint tourist port for some passenger ships as well.

What a sight it was. We approached through the fiord-like harbor entrance in semi-darkness at 9:30 A.M. The ship, almost hidden in blinding snow, crawled through the narrow channel toward the port like a huge white panther stalking an invisible prey, inching ever closer, until suddenly the dock magically appeared close by. *Nice job, Captain!*

As daylight filtered through the snow, the edge of the town emerged, speckled with wood frame houses perched on nearby hills among tall fir trees, lights twinkling like welcome beacons. Four inches of fresh white stuff already covered the ground. On the pier below, cabs and buses waited to shuttle our passengers to the airport. No wind. Cold. Quiet, except for the sound of falling snow, like a soft ringing in your ears. No hoopla. No horns. No shouting. No confusion. Calm. Organized. Patient. How Norwegian.

Three hours later we were on our way into the North Sea. It was a little rough, but not too bad, 20-foot seas and winds at 20 knots. A few minor hiccups punctuated production show rehearsals. Due to the rolling but not violent seas, a few of the sets, as yet unsecured, moved in and out across the stage, making unscheduled entrances, not unusual for a new ship. With twenty or so large scenic sets to install, it takes time to secure them all properly. You don't notice unsecured ones until the heavy seas quickly tell you which they are. The group had a good laugh each time a set would roll onto the stage like a phantom, and we'd then take the time to lock it down. Excitement was high among the show cast of fourteen and our production installation team of forty.

During the night the seas calmed and the weather cleared. I woke up at 3:30 A.M., looked out my sliding glass doors and saw several brightly lit North Sea oil rigs about three miles off the starboard side, looming there like ominous, giant *War of the Worlds* machines. I couldn't imagine being a rig worker living on those things—miles from nowhere, out in one of the most turbulent bodies of water on the planet. How gutsy.

On the fourth day we passed through the English Channel and cleared France and Spain, passing by the Bay of Biscay. The seas were flat. Someone could probably have water-skied off the stern. We were cutting along at about 22 knots, already having covered over 1,500 miles since Finland. All seemed smooth as we headed southwest toward Florida.

One night the captain announced that a large storm was moving toward us from the coast of America. "Too large to avoid." I accelerated our work schedule in the Theatre and the ice rink, in the event we had to batten down later.

We managed to avoid the main storm—a huge one, perhaps a thousand miles across. But we had to pass through its outer fringes. That was enough. I was ready and anxious to see how the big ship handled the weather.

As we got closer to the storm, the seas kept building. By four in the afternoon the waves were 30 to 35 feet, long swells with a surly chop. Our course took us right into the wind. With gusts kicking in at 40 to 45 knots, our forward speed was about 15 knots, so the relative wind over the deck was around 60 knots. Not exactly your stroll-around-the-deck breeze. It was bumpy. We called off rehearsals. Several of the dancers were already seasick, especially the first-time ocean-crossers. It is a miserable feeling. You want to die. Some of them looked close to it.

Every time the huge ship collided with a big swell, the ocean spray kicked up from the impact and flew past my windows in huge billowing white plumes. These reached well above my Deck 6 cabin—about the height of a six-story building. Really beautiful Kodak-moment stuff.

An hour later, holding tightly to the main stairway railing, I made my way down to the theatre lobby again. At times both feet were off the stairs. On Deck 4, closer to the sea, I looked out the glass doors that led to the outside Promenade deck. Several hearty folks were in the lobby also, oohing and ahhing over the seas and big sprays. We were doing our sea-legs thing, bobbing and lurching and shifting weight from one leg to the other, knees flexed, riding the swells like snow skiers. It was fun.

An ominous cloudbank was moving across the water toward us. It stretched out as far as we could see and looked like a summertime squall line that comes up suddenly and sweeps across Long Island Sound or Biscayne Bay or the Chesapeake. It wasn't a dark cloudbank, but more of an opaque gray with a definite leading edge. The distance between the cloud and the ship closed rapidly until suddenly it was upon us.

It was rain. Heavy rain. It settled onto the sea around us, pelting the turbulence with billions of beebee-like drops. It was strange. It smothered the white caps, flattened their tops and muted the chop, as if a huge pillow were stifling the tops of angry waves. All the while the big rolling swells continued. The rain was actually beating up on the ocean!

The effect was beautiful and a little spooky. For a moment I could imagine we were in one of those Twilight Zone-Bermuda Triangle things, where a large ship is enveloped in a strange time-warp cloud, mysteriously finding itself back in the middle of World War II.

But it was not to be. The phenomenon lasted only fifteen minutes or so. The cloud passed, the rain stopped, and the sea kicked in again. Only now it seemed angrier at having been stifled by the sudden rain attack. The fierce chop seemed invigorated.

A half hour later an announcement came from the bridge. It was the captain. The ship had to be stopped. Everyone was to prepare to hold on securely. All public rooms were closed.

Elevators were shut down—the ship had twelve passenger lifts and several for crew. All activities ceased. A ship does not stop in high seas unless it's absolutely necessary. The seas were rough, but nothing close to hurricane force, which this ship could well take. We speculated there might be engine trouble. We hoped not.

Soon the ship stopped and began drifting backward. Oddly, things calmed down because we were now floating with the waves and the wind. At that rate I figured we'd be swept back to Spain in three days.

Several minutes later we were underway again, making forward speed. The pounding resumed as we again rammed into the seas. We found out later that one of the two stabilizers had fouled in the formidable waves.

Stabilizers are 25-foot-long wings that can be extended out from the sides underwater near the bow to stabilize the ship in rough weather. The only way the captain could retract them was to stop all forward power, drift backwards, reducing resistance, then withdraw the stabilizers. It worked. The wings were retracted for repair, and off we went again, bouncing and jitterbugging across the ocean. *Nice ride.* Very little damage to the ship. A few bar glasses took a dive, but not much else. A most interesting couple of days. The sea was full of surprises.

We made up for the four hours we'd lost in mid-Atlantic rough seas. The ship was making 22 to 23 knots now. Arrival in Miami was scheduled to be on time.

One night near the end of our fourteen-day trip, I woke up at 3:00 A.M. I went outside onto my cabin's balcony. The sea was asleep. We were skimming along like a giant porpoise.

Overhead a dome of millions of stars, from horizon to horizon, hovered over us like a huge glowing half-globe, softly illuminated the ocean. With no ambient light, the heavens really light up. Stars you never knew were there say hello. And the more you stare, the more there are. You just can't see them all. It was peaceful.

The sun finally did its "I'm back" thing—the first time in two weeks. Temperatures rose into the 70s, and the steely gray ocean was blue again. We were nearly back to the States. The crew was anticipating getting to Miami soon. Many of them were foreign nationals and had never been to America. Some, especially the young Russian ice skaters, told me they were really anxious and excited to see South Beach! Now that's America. Hmm.

All in all, it was an excellent voyage for the new behemoth, *The Navigator of the Seas*, as it sailed the 5,000 miles to its new home in Miami. It had been a privilege to be a part of its beginning and to do this one more time. The voyage was an eye opener for me in more ways than one.

Another change was coming.

During my tenure at Royal Caribbean I wrote a second collection of poetry and published a book of poems for tennis hackers, *Going To Court*. The project allowed me to satisfy a different creative inclination and supported my love of the sport. I loved the writing process and was pleased with the results of the book. Later I wrote several short stories, began a memoir, and decided to study creative writing when time permitted in the creative writing program of Florida International University in Miami. It was a new beginning. Another world was opening up.

When I entered the cruise industry as a former musician I couldn't have envisioned a new career being so stimulating and productive, both professionally and personally. Frankly, I was amazed at my luck. The golden age of exponential growth of cruising and of building super-colossal ships beyond reasonable imagination—ships three to four times the size of the Titanic—was at hand, and I was fortunate to be part of it.

During those dynamic times I observed a plethora of corporate intrigues and ship-related adventures, many interesting enough to fill at least another volume. Perhaps the account of the twenty odd years I spent in the cruise industry will evolve into another memoir, one about life after music, behind-the-scenes on board today's super cruise ships.

Or maybe not. Maybe music is more than something you once did. Maybe it's the part of you that never dies.

*

And so another ocean was crossed. The transition was made to a new life. You were born again. And they all lived happily ever after. Tsk, tsk.

(Oh, give it a rest. Why don't you write your own memoir?)

Huh?

**

Twenty Four

CODA

Many classical works of music summarize themes and add new sparks, as a coda, or tail, brings the piece to a close. With this in mind, I add these thoughts that tell the tail, or tail the tale, if you prefer...

Driving to the cruise line office one morning, I heard the FM jazz station announcer say "And that was the Duke Ellington Orchestra at the 1962 Newport Jazz Festival."

There had to be a mistake. No recordings of the '62 Festival were ever released, since the master tapes were all defective. I was curious and called the station.

"Yes," they insisted, "that was Duke Ellington at the 1962 Newport Jazz Festival."

"Are you sure it was 1962?"

"Yes, sir."

They had apparently picked up the program from a New York City FM outlet. But when I contacted that station, no one seemed to know anything about the Duke Ellington 1962 Newport recording. One person suggested that the Festival's live overseas broadcast via Armed Forces Radio was probably recorded in Germany.

So began a surprising series of events that caught me unaware and unprepared.

Thirty-five years after the *Jazz Giants* performance at Newport '62, one of life's ironies—which seem to delight in staging capricious appearances—made a surprise entrance. This time the ripple effect morphed into a wave that did not sputter and disappear like a spent flood on a beach.

The search began to verify the radio broadcast. The trail led to the Rutgers University Institute for Jazz Studies, where I sought information from anyone who would listen to me. At someone's suggestion, I then tried to contact a well-known jazz writer at *Downbeat Magazine*, writing and calling him several times. No response. The trail that had warmed so quickly suddenly cooled.

I gave up the search and set it aside as just another near miss. Though a disappointment, it seemed no tragedy to me. You can't lose what you've never had.

At our annual Christmas-in-Connecticut family reunion that year, I told the story to my family, suggesting that if there were Festival recordings of Ellington in '62, it was possible that the *Jazz Giants* had been recorded there also.

"Not that it would make any difference now," I said. "But wouldn't it be interesting if the story were true? Oh well, we'll never know." But silently I mused on what might have happened if the past had been different—if the *Jazz Giants* had released a best-selling international album back then.

Five years passed. Early in 2003, more than forty years since Newport, Peter, one of my four sons, called me from Connecticut more excited than I had heard him since he was a spirited two-year-old who gleefully discovered the sheer joy of banging pots and pans together in the kitchen at six o'clock in the morning.

I didn't know it at the time, but ever since I had mentioned hearing Duke's live recording, Peter had been quietly trying to track it down. He was on a mission. He had heard part of a National Public Radio announcement saying the Library of Congress was making available to the public thousands of heretofore inaccessible jazz recordings it had acquired and catalogued. He started digging.

Now the wave, almost ashore a few years before, only to dissipate, was building again. This time it would smack into me with an impact I couldn't have imagined. Phone calls and letters were exchanged, request forms filled out. Peter finally received the answer. No wonder he was excited when he called me. I was amazed.

In addition to Ellington, the Library of Congress had in its archives a tape of "The Gene Hull Orchestra, The *Jazz Giants*, at Newport '62." A single CD could be assembled from the tape and made available with permission of the producer, George Wein. His office staff graciously assisted Peter in his quest, approving a CD for him with their blessing "for non-commercial purposes only."

"Dad," said Peter, "I'm going to get those recordings for you. It's going to be your birthday present this year."

Not really, I thought, not after all these years. "Thanks for trying. But don't count on it. It's been so long. Anything could happen."

The news startled me. It made me recall so many forgotten journeys. I tried to convince myself some history should remain buried, that some things really don't matter anymore. The truth was I wasn't sure I wanted to hear the recordings for fear they wouldn't live up to my memories. And what difference would it make now anyway? After all, I wasn't a musician any longer, so it really didn't matter to me. Or did it?

Would I be disillusioned hearing the recordings after so many years? Perhaps our Newport performance was, after all, just another gig along the way. We all choose our memories and the way we want to remember them. I wondered if my memories of Newport would have to be reshaped. I could see the visuals of that day clearly, but the sounds that filled the night had gradually faded.

The *Jazz Giants* had been engrossing for me, as were the years spent with my other bands. I was always determined to develop and hone a first-class, professional product. It took a colossal amount of time and energy. Sometimes I regretted the commitment. But the early promise to succeed, many years before, a promise born of pride and desire for accomplishment, would not tolerate being broken. I persisted in pursuing a career in music.

As I considered these thoughts, Peter continued digging and subsequently received the CD from the Library of Congress.

Finally, in July 2003, Peter chose a family reunion in Hingham, Massachusetts at my son Matthew's home to present the recording to me. Many of the family were grouped around the kitchen table to watch the big moment.

Just looking at the packaged CD placed before me gave me a jolt like a sudden electric current. Shivers came right from the stomach. Then I completely lost it.

"Dad, my daughter Amy whispered, "why are you crying? "I've never seen you cry."

"I don't know."

But I did know. I was seeing my yesterdays. My grown children as wide-eyed little kids, asking me where I was going. And me telling them, "Straight up." The *Jazz Giants* rehearsing at Bill's Castle. A boy sitting on a bus on a cold winter night, clutching his first saxophone wrapped in a pillow case. All the jazz concerts the band had played. Katherine Hepburn scolding me. Benny Goodman captivating me. Paul Whiteman berating

GENE HULL

me. Woody Herman and Duke Ellington making me feel humble. Las Vegas dazzling and disappointing me. The years with Damone. Elvis greeting me with such honesty. The miles of piled-up travel. And saying good-bye to a teary young family and wife on the front porch, as I'd leave to seek fame and fortune on yet another road trip.

Being a musician came with a price. Either I hadn't realized the possible collateral damage such dedication could do to my family, or I knew it, and thought I could repair it, once I had made it. It had been a gamble. At the time it seemed like a logical risk. Such decisions depend on things that live only in your own head.

Crossroad choices are certainly influenced by early-seeded emotions. The need for a constantly replenished sense of self-worth is the entertainer's curse. And I'm sure I'm not the only one who has experienced it. The quest for self-affirmation can drive one to the limit.

I tried to tell my family that this CD was more than just a recording, that their lives were in it as much as mine. It didn't matter that I couldn't find the words. They knew.

We listened to the CD together. The sound of the band, with its energy and musicality, far exceeded the memories I had parked away. Now suddenly the sounds were alive and bright again, clearer than ever.

The look on their faces was worth the struggling years. The kids understood at last why the *Jazz Giants* had been one of the most important musical accomplishments of my life, and appreciated what it took to create it.

David and Chris, both professional musicians, said they had no idea the level of musicianship of the *Giants* was of that caliber, and were genuinely impressed. Matt, a former musician, was wide-eyed at the sound. Becca, Margaret and Sara hugged me with the shared joy only daughters can give their fathers.

Peter, also a musician, personally delivered a copy of the recording to each of the surviving members of the *Jazz Giants*. Originally there were twenty musicians. Twelve were still living. He said the response from them in most every case was at first disbelief, then shock, followed by profuse thanks and finally tears of joy.

Ron Gebeau, clearly surprised, was speechless. He couldn't believe it. Tears filled his eyes as he kept staring at the CD. Mickey Walker was astonished and clearly overwhelmed. "Are you kidding me, man? This is unbelievable." He telephoned me in Florida to tell me how extraordinary it was, and what a wonderful son I had. Bobby Butler praised Peter and proclaimed the CD one of the most appreciated gifts of his lifetime. Danny DeMarco at first was speechless, then, wet-eyed, hardly able to get the words out, said, "Oh man, so many years..." Freddie Fortunato and Al Provensano both wrote glowing letters of thanks to me. Others voiced similar effusements.

I need to take a moment here to remember the fine young men who were members of the *Jazz Giants* over the years. Leo Grabinski, Nick Mariconda, Sonny Costanzo, Jeff Leonard, Joe Howard, Tommy Alberts, Glen Zatola, Bobby Zatola, Dick Prestige, Claude Berardi, Bobby Harry, Harry Ashmore, Bruce Powers, Ricky Bruno, Jack Corso, Bobby Butler, Dom Mariconda, Joe Marzulli, Danny DeMarco, Danny Acrotta, Peter Daddario, Tony Guzzi, Fred Fortunato, Mickey Walker, Jack Spake, Bob Nolting, Joe Daddona, Steve Royal, Ronnie Gebeau, Dick Burlant, Al Provenzano, Sheldon Rose, Steve Powers, Marty Rose and Robert Foster. *Gentlemen, you were dedicated. You were the best.*

For some the *Jazz Giants* had marked a musical zenith in their lives. It meant more to them than they cared to admit at the time. But when those who played at Newport received the CD package that recaptured their musical accomplishment of over forty years ago, the emotions poured out. What they did back then still mattered to them, just as it did to me. And that is the most surprising aspect of the whole music saga.

In looking back on the music career, which I have seldom done – most always focused on the 'now' – except when it was essential in writing a memoir, I realize I have been one of the lucky people in life who has known first-hand the heady experience of communicating real emotions, feelings and ideas through the unique language of music.

No matter how the profession of musician is sometimes regarded by some of the establishment, such work matters to society; it is a gift, without which there would be no music. And that's the point. I can't imagine such a world. Making music is one of life's important endeavors, not to be taken for granted—especially by musicians themselves. Many marvelous musicians, far more accomplished than I, have made such lasting contributions. For this they deserve our respect.

As for myself, even though I have long since recovered from the fascinating grip of making music, I will always cherish the experience.

And that's the truth, so help me, Charlie Parker.

*

How sweet. Was that a sermon?

(Oh stuff it.)

* * * *

WITH GRATITUDE

It takes a bit of bravado to contemplate writing a memoir. You have to believe that what has happened in your life may be interesting enough for others to want to read about. it. For me, this took some convincing. So I thank those who maintained that I had story worth telling and encouraged me to do so.

During this writing process I discovered much about my life I hadn't realized before. For that alone I am grateful.

I sincerely thank those who helped me keep these memoirs on track during the long draft-and-revision process.

In particular I thank Susan Parsons, whose initial and steady encouragement to write a memoir started me working on it, and my wife Beverly, whose conceptual insights proved most helpful.

Various readers have had important input at various stages of the drafts, especially Becca Herst, Patty Buendia, Amy Hull, Todd Williams, Margaret Spencer, Beverly Myers-Hull, Lenore Mascar, Darina Prodanova, Sara MacKay, David Hull, Mary Read, Calvin Herst, Chris Hull, and Senior Editor Mary Moby of A-I Editing for her critique of the first completed draft.

I am grateful, too, for the helpful suggestions of the members of the Martin County Writers Association, the Morningside Writers Group, and particularly Leona Bodie, Diane Desrouchers, Jane Marshall and Barbara Samuels of the Treasure Coast Word Weavers. To all of you and others whom I may have missed, I give my sincere thanks.

Gene

GENE HULL

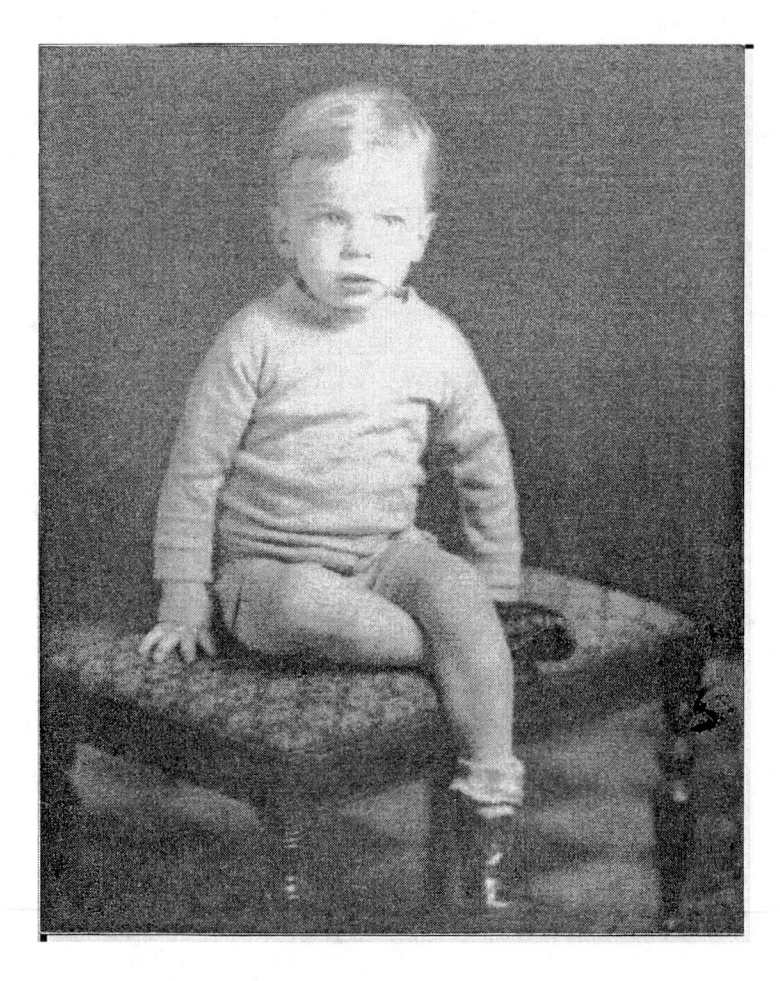

Portrait of a musician-to-be at age two.

ABOUT THE AUTHOR

Born in Bridgeport, Connecticut, Gene Hull is a former big band saxophonist, symphony clarinetist and jazz flutist. He was musical director for many celebrity performers, leader of the *Jazz Giants, Free Spirit, GK-3, and Music Maximus*. After a lengthy musical career, he became the entertainment producer for Royal Caribbean Cruises' award-winning production shows.

Gene attended the Juilliard School, graduated from Fairfield College Preparatory School, is a music graduate of the University of Notre Dame, and studied in the Creative Writing Program at Florida International University. He is the proud and grateful father of eight children—four daughters and four sons, three of whom are professional musicians. Writing is now his full-time avocation. His third book, a collection of short stories, *The Runner* is scheduled to be published in Spring, 2007.

He and his wife Beverly reside on Florida's Treasure Coast with their Mini Schnauzer *Coda*.

GENE HULL

HOOKED ON A HORN may be ordered on line through www.genehull.com, Amazon.com, Borders.com, Trafford.com, Barnes & Noble.com and selected retailers. Gene can been reached at genehull@msn.com and welcomes your comments.

Award Winning Cover Design by
RORY MYERS, Rory Myers Design Group,
Brooklyn , NY

POST SCRIPT

As this second edition of "HOOKED A ON A HORN" went to press, *Aerosmith* invited bassist DAVID HULL, Gene's oldest son, to join the group for its 2006 fall tour. During this time David replaced Tom Hamilton, Rock and Roll Hall of Famer, the group's regular bassist since 1970.

Along with *The Rolling Stones* and *U-2, Aerosmith* is one of the world's foremost and durable rock bands, and features lead singer Steven Tyler.

David, a well-known bassist, has played and recorded with many famous rock groups worldwide over the years. He is a long-time friend of *Aerosmith* band members.

If anything could make this father happier for his son, he can't imagine what it could be. As a famous couple once sang so infectiously, "The Beat Goes On."

Finally, one last thing. Many people have asked to hear the *Newport '62* recording of the *Jazz Giants,* here-to-fore unavailable. The author is pleased to report that this rare "lost recording"—retrieved from in the archives of the Library of Congress—is now available through the author's website.

**

ISBN 141206721-9